THE PROFESSIONAL
NURSE AND THE LAW

THE PROFESSIONAL NURSE AND THE LAW

Daniel A. Rothman, J.D.

Nancy Lloyd Rothman, R.N., B.S.N., M.Ed.

Instructor, Gwynedd Mercy College
Gwynedd Valley, Pennsylvania

Little, Brown and Company
Boston

Copyright © 1977 by Daniel A. Rothman
and Nancy Lloyd Rothman

First Edition

All rights reserved. No part of this book may be
reproduced in any form or by any electronic or
mechanical means, including information
storage and retrieval systems, without
permission in writing from the publisher, except
by a reviewer who may quote brief
passages in a review.

Library of Congress Catalog Card
No. 76-52624

ISBN 0-316-75768-3

Printed in the United States of America

83766

To Our Children,
Edie and Danny

PREFACE

We have attempted to meet the need for a readily understandable text on the legal aspects of nursing. We have not attempted to provide a "do it yourself" book on legal problems or a substitute for professional legal services. Nor have we attempted to provide a definitive reference book on any of the fields of law. In a text of this size, such an effort would have been patently impossible. We have tried to provide a readable text tracing the broad outlines of those areas of law of particular concern to nurses. Of necessity, some of the fields of law discussed in this book are of general interest to any person concerned with his or her rights and obligations. Many chapters, such as those dealing with torts, nurse practice acts, consumerism and accountability, collective bargaining, national health care, death, and principles for nurses to remember, are of primary concern to nurses.

We hope our readers enjoy using this book as much as we enjoyed writing it. If they have only a small part of the patience that our two young children, Edie and Danny, displayed while their parents worked on this book, we are sure they will find its use rewarding and instructive.

The nursing profession will never achieve the status it deserves unless nurses are willing to assume the responsibility for guiding its growth through progressive legislation and role change. For this task it is essential that nurses know their legal rights and obligations.

Dresher, Pennsylvania   D.A.R.
                                                              N.L.R.

CONTENTS

THE PROFESSIONAL
NURSE AND THE LAW

1. PROPERTY RIGHTS

Human beings enter the world with certain deep-seated primal instincts. Among these are the desire for food, shelter, and love, and freedom from pain, injury, and death. These instincts are not necessarily compatible with living in an ordered society or in a densely populated area. Human beings attained their ascendancy on this planet not through their brute strength, but through their intellect and their capability for collective action. This ascendancy was only possible because of the ability of the human race to coordinate its activities and live in more or less ordered societies.

An ordered society is, by implication, a society with rules and standards of conduct for its members, defining their goals and setting guidelines and limitations for the fulfillment of their basic primitive drives. Broadly stated, the rules and standards of society that control the conduct of its individual members and set limitations and guidelines for the fulfillment of natural impulses are called laws. These laws may be imposed by a despot who rules through strength and fear without the consent of those governed, by an elected body governing with the consent of those governed, by long-standing custom and practice, or by a combination of these and other means.

The society in which the readers of this book will live their lives is extremely complex. Their day-to-day conduct is governed by a body of law that encompasses and controls every aspect of their lives. It has been said that the law is a "seamless web" and this is, in fact, an apt metaphor since the law envelops our activities, prospects, and aspirations from birth to death and, in some respects, thereafter as well.

Without laws and without a society under law, we would have anarchy, or what has otherwise been called the law of the jungle. The strongest would prevail in every situation. People would only survive to the extent that they could defend their own lives and bodies, and they would only own property to the extent that they could physically defend it against those who wished to take it from them. At an early stage in his development, man determined that this was not the way to live. What then are these laws that govern our lives and envelop us like a cocoon or the air we breathe? A law is a rule applicable to the members of society for the purpose of recognizing a particular interest of the government of that society or of its individual members.

To be more specific, a law that makes certain types of killing a crime recognizes the right of the individual members of society to be free from murderous assaults. Another law that provides for the imposition of taxes

1

recognizes the collective interest of the members of a society in having services that its government can provide and the interest of the government in having a method to pay for these services. A law that governs the disposition of the estates of decedents recognizes the interest and desire of most individuals to provide for the disposition of their assets on their death. Preeminent among the interests recognized and protected by laws is the *general interest* in an ordered society without which we would have anarchy and a situation in which only the strongest would survive.

Another way of approaching the law is in terms of rights. When an individual has an interest that society recognizes and protects it may be said that he has a right. For instance, individuals have an interest in owning real estate and being reasonably free from the interference of others in the enjoyment of that ownership. If this interest is recognized and protected by the state it may be said that they have a *right* to such ownership [1]. The ability to acquire, own, and dispose of property is the cornerstone of an ordered and civilized society.

PROPERTY DEFINED

What is property? In a sense it only exists by virtue of laws. While a lay person may think of property in terms of real estate, which is land or things permanently attached to land, or in terms of personal property, which consists of all the other movable things in the world capable of being owned, a lawyer thinks of property as a collection of rights. Therefore, a lawyer might say that a person owns something only to the extent that he has a legal interest in it that is recognized and protected by society in the form of a law.

Stated another way, a person who lives on a piece of land does not own it unless society, for one reason or another, recognizes his right to quiet enjoyment of that land. Ownership may be of varying degrees, starting with ownership *in fee simple*, or absolute ownership, which gives the owner the right to use a piece of land for any lawful use that does not unreasonably interfere with rights of his neighbors, to sell or lease his land, and to dispose of it by a will at his death. These rights are frequently divisible. For instance, a person owning a piece of land may sell one portion of it, occupy another portion, and lease a third portion. The laws applying to interests in land, sometimes called real property, vary in many respects from those dealing with personal or movable property [2].

Both real and personal property may be owned, but a piece of land is truly unique. While the law recognizes the fact that a person who is unlawfully deprived of an item of personal property may be compensated in money damages, laws involving real estate often provide for the restoration of a particular piece of land to its rightful owner. This distinction can be traced to the feudal system, in which the ownership of land was the basis of the entire social and economic order.

Personal property is divided into two broad categories: tangibles and intangibles. Tangible personal property encompasses things that can be seen, touched, and moved, such as automobiles, coins, watches, and books. Another class of personal property consists of transferable rights against other persons. Lawyers call these intangible items of personal property *choses in action*. A chose in action could be a check, which is a right to collect money from a bank; a stock certificate, which is evidence of ownership of a portion of a corporation; a bank deposit book, or even a lease. Rights in personal property also may be acquired, enjoyed, divided, lost, and transferred [3].

ACQUISITION OF PROPERTY
Most of us spend the greater portion of our lives in an attempt to acquire property, things which bring comfort, security, and a certain unique life style to ourselves and our families, things which we can obviously not take with us to whatever we believe to be the next world. In this intensive quest for property, spiritual and ethical goals and values are often neglected or ignored.

Since this book is not intended as a treatise on ethics and religion, we will not dwell at any great length on the relative merits of this acquisitive point of view. Suffice it to say that much of the present high standard of living to which citizens of the Western democracies have become accustomed is based on acquisition and possession of private property.

How may this property be acquired, or, stated another way, how may an individual acquire an interest in things or in land that would be recognized and protected by society? One way is by acquiring possession of a thing or piece of land that belongs to no one else. Except for an occasional uncharted atoll, very little land on this earth still fits that description, so we may reasonably omit unclaimed land from this discussion. However, items of personal property (as opposed to real property) with no owner are still plentiful. One obvious example is wild game. While the owner of the piece of land on which a hunter acquires possession of a wild animal has a greater claim to the animal than the hunter, the hunter has a greater claim than everyone else. Furthermore, a person hunting on a game preserve, or on his own land, has title to a captured or slain wild animal that is good against the whole world. Goods and things may be abandoned; that is, their prior owner may relinquish control of the goods or things with the intention of permanently divesting himself of ownership. One who acquires possession of such an item becomes its new owner [4].

Lost Property
The situation is different in the case of lost goods. If an item is lost, the one who finds it and obtains control over it has greater title to it than everyone except the original owner who may reclaim it [5]. The situation is also

different in the case of misplaced goods. An item that has been misplaced must be distinguished from an item that is lost. When one deliberately places an item in a particular place and forgets the location of the item, it has been misplaced; whereas, if an item is inadvertently dropped and not found, it is lost. The one who finds an item that has been misplaced has title to it that is superior to that of everyone but the owner of the premises on which the item was found and, of course, the original owner [6].

For example, someone who picked up a lamp or some other piece of household furnishing left on the curb by a householder for the garbage men would have better title to that item than anyone else. A nurse who found a wrist watch in a rest room in a hospital, which had been placed on the sink by another nurse who was washing her hands, would have found a misplaced item and would have a good title against everyone but the hospital and the original owner of the watch. However, if the same watch were found by the same nurse in the hall with the strap broken so that it was apparent that it had fallen from its original owner's wrist, the nurse who found it would have good title against everyone but the original owner since the watch would have been lost.

Gifts

Another highly esteemed and universally applauded way of acquiring property is by gift. A gift, by its nature, involves the transfer of property to the recipient without payment or a quid pro quo of any kind. Generally, it denotes esteem or affection on the part of the giver for the recipient, but this is of no legal consequence. How does one make a gift? What is necessary in order to accomplish this transfer of legally protected rights to an item so as to vest them in the recipient of the gift? First, there must be the intention to make a gift or *donative intent*. The donative intent must be a present intent. Intent to make a gift in the future will not suffice. In order for the gift-giving to be consummated there must be a present intent to make a transfer of the rights of the donor in a particular item to the recipient. In addition, there must be delivery, which represents a transfer of possession of the item to be given from the donor to the recipient. In the case of a small item, such as a watch or a coin, the act of transferring possession is easy to understand. With some larger items, such as automobiles, the transfer of possession may be constructive or symbolic, for example, the delivery of keys. In any event, the transfer of possession or delivery may be accomplished by a formal, written instrument or deed signed by the donor. Another requirement for a valid gift, which is perhaps too obvious to require much attention, is acceptance by the recipient. Obviously, a gift may be refused for any reason and, in most cases, in the face of such refusal, delivery is impossible.

TESTAMENTARY GIFTS. Testamentary gifts are another very important category of gift. They involve gifts which take effect on the death of the donor. In the United States, and in most other countries, testamentary gifts must be in writing and signed by the donor [7]. This document is referred to generally as a will or testament, and lawyers refer to the giver in such cases as the testator in the case of a man and the testatrix in the case of a woman. Wills and the disposition of decedents' estates are a matter for serious consideration by the professional nurse, not only because she is mortal and may wish to provide for the disposition of her worldly goods at the time of her own death, but also because she frequently deals with people who, reminded of their own mortality by illness and infirmity, may wish her to witness a will or obtain for them the services of a lawyer [8]. Frequently the mental condition of such individuals as it bears on their capacity to make a will may be an issue before a court of law, and the nurse's testimony may be required.

GIFTS A CAUSA MORTIS. Gifts made in anticipation of imminent death from an existing infirmity are given special treatment by the law. They are known as gifts *a causa mortis*. Like testamentary gifts, the subject of gifts a causa mortis may be of particular interest to nurses. A nurse could conceivably be the recipient of such a gift and, like anyone else, she might at some time in her life wish to make such a gift. Of course, she could be called into court to testify regarding such gift-giving she observed in the course of performing her professional duties.

In order for a gift to be treated as a gift a causa mortis, the giver, while not necessarily about to die, must believe that his or her death is imminent from an existing infirmity. An example would be a man who was about to have a serious operation that he was not sure he would survive. If, under such circumstances, he gives a piece of jewelry or some other object to a friend and actually delivers it to him or transfers it to him by means of a signed, written document, such a gift would be treated as a gift in contemplation of death or a gift a causa mortis and could be revoked under certain circumstances.

In general, it may said that the survival of the contemplated peril, of itself, revokes a gift a causa mortis. Therefore, in the case we are discussing, if the man survived the operation he could reclaim the jewelry at any time during his lifetime or, after his later death, it could be claimed by his executor as part of his estate.

The death of the recipient of the gift a causa mortis prior to the death of the person making the gift operates as a revocation of the gift, and the original donor may then reclaim the gift.

It is obvious that such gifts may be the subject of fraud. A great deal of litigation has taken place regarding the circumstances of gifts in contemplation of death. It is very possible that a nurse at some time in her career might be called into court to testify in regard to the circumstances of a gift a causa mortis, in order to help the court determine the actual intention of the donor [9].

Acquisition of Property by Contract

The most common method of transferring property between individuals in our society is by a binding agreement between the seller and the buyer of the object sold. The field of contracts is extremely complex and is the subject of a great body of judicial opinions and legal texts; it is also one of the most important courses in a law school. It will suffice for the purpose of this book to say that for a promise to be binding it must be supported by consideration; that is, in general, the promisor must receive something of value for the promise.

A promise given in return for another promise is sufficient to constitute a contract enforceable in a court of law. This is frequently the type of contract involved in a sale.

For instance, the buyer promises to pay an agreed sum of money for a specific object in return for which the seller agrees to transfer ownership of the object to the buyer. This type of agreement is frequently not pronounced in formal legal language by the parties to it, but rather is implied by their actions. For example, a woman might go into a dress shop and select a dress on which the price is clearly marked. She says to the salesperson, "I'll take it." In so doing, she has accepted the offer of the store to sell the dress for the price indicated and has promised to pay that price in return for the transfer of ownership of the dress.

Lawyers sometimes refer to such transactions as offer and acceptance, the offer being the promise to sell for a given price, and the acceptance being the promise to pay the price. Such an agreement is a binding contract based on a promise for a promise. Obviously, the promises must be in identically corresponding terms. For example, if the woman who was looking at the dresses selected a dress marked $50 and offered to pay $25 for it, there would be no contract since the two promises were in different terms. Until the proprietor of the store agreed to accept $25 for the dress, there would be no sale.

The second essential ingredient of a transfer of property by sale is ownership of the property by the seller. With few exceptions, a person who does not own an object himself cannot give ownership or title to that object to another. There is then an obvious conflict of interest between buyers who buy goods in good faith from sellers who do not have title to them and the true owners of the goods, who may wish to reclaim them. It is one of those conflicts that cannot be resolved in a completely satisfactory manner with full justice done to all the parties involved.

In the British Commonwealth the doctrine of *market overt* is followed, which means that in the case of goods sold in fairs, marketplaces, and stores, the good faith purchaser has better title to stolen goods than their true owner.

In the United States, the doctrine of market overt has never been popular, and the true owner of stolen goods prevails over the good faith purchaser [10]. However, even in the United States there are certain important exceptions to the rule that the true owner of stolen goods prevails over the good faith purchaser:

1. The first and most important of these is in the case of currency. Obviously, it would be impossible for the economy and commerce of our country to survive if everyone who received money in payment of a debt had to determine that the source of the money was indeed the person making the payment. The basic characteristic of currency is that it is freely circulated and accepted without question as payment for all legal debts. Therefore, currency, whether in the form of coins or bank notes, cannot be recovered by its rightful owner once it has passed in payment of a lawful debt or for a valuable consideration as part of a contract. Before it has thus passed, the true owner can recover it in a legal action for the money itself.

2. The same rule that applies to currency has been extended to a class of documents representing choses in action. As the reader will recall, choses in action are legal rights against an individual or institution, such as the right of ownership a shareholder has in a corporation, which is represented by his stock certificate, or the right to payment from a bank, represented by a check or draft. Certain of these choses in action are represented by documents designed to be passed freely in commerce without a written endorsement. An example would be a check or a bank note payable to bearer or endorsed in blank, each of which is designed to pass freely in commercial intercourse. Lawyers refer to such documents as negotiable instruments. A purchaser in good faith of such a negotiable instrument, who has no notice of a defect in a seller's title, will prevail against a claim of the true owner if the instrument has in fact been stolen or obtained by fraud by the seller [11].

WHEN DOES TITLE PASS? Frequently a buyer and a seller enter into an agreement of sale, and before the object sold is actually delivered, it is destroyed or damaged. Who bears the burden of the loss? Did the ownership of the object sold remain in the seller until the time of delivery, or did the buyer become the owner at the time of the original agreement? This question has been the subject of a great deal of litigation in the courts, and the rules for determining the exact moment that ownership or title passes are complex and subject to many exceptions and variations.

For the purposes of this book, it is sufficient to point out the general rule that title passes at the time the parties intend it to pass, and their intent may be determined from all the circumstances of the sale, including the contract itself. For instance, if the contract for the sale of a particular item or particular goods already in existence calls for delivery by the seller to the buyer at a particular place, the title to the goods and the risk of loss does not pass to the buyer until the time of actual delivery, regardless of whether the goods have been actually paid for or not.

For example, a woman ordering a particular dress from a department store that agrees to deliver it to her house would not be responsible for payment for the dress if it were destroyed by fire before the time of actual delivery. However, a man who purchased a chair at a furniture store and who agreed to stop by with a truck the next day and pick it up would have ownership of the chair immediately on the agreement of the sale, and if the chair were destroyed by fire before he actually picked it up he would still be responsible for payment of the purchase price.

In another situation, if an individual visited a lumber yard and ordered a certain amount of lumber that was not then and there specifically identified and allocated to his purchase, and said he would pick it up the next day or at some subsequent time, he would not bear the risk of loss if the lumber yard burned down before the specific lumber had been allocated to his purchase.

The variations in the possible factual situations are infinite and this text is not the place to discuss all the possible variations and exceptions, it being sufficient for the reader to know that they exist.

Transfer of Ownership by Judicial Decree

Under certain circumstances courts have the power to transfer ownership rights in specific goods by judicial decree. In a sense, the courts are merely determining pre-existing rights rather than creating new ones. To the extent that the judgment of a court having jurisdiction over the parties and the subject matter is final, even though it might be erroneous, its determination of the ownership of particular goods or land creates property rights.

In general, when two parties dispute the ownership of a particular object, the judgment of the court is binding only as to those parties. Lawyers call such a judgment a judgment *in personam*, or one that is binding only on the individuals actually party to the litigation that resulted in the decree. Take for example the case of a woman who claims to have purchased a valuable antique for a modest price and an antique dealer who denies that he had ever made such a contract. If they decide to dispute the matter in court, the resulting judicial decree determining who owns the particular antique will be binding as to the two of them, but not as to other persons not party to the litigation. For instance, a third individual may claim to be the true owner of the antique, and allege that the antique dealer obtained its possession by fraud.

In certain other cases, courts enter decrees determining ownership of things or land as to the whole world. The resulting judgments are known as judgments *in rem*. A common example of this is an action to *quiet title*. When ownership of a particular piece of land is in doubt, one who claims good title may bring an action to quiet title in a court of proper jurisdiction. Thereafter, notice of the action is served on all parties known to claim an interest in the land and also on the rest of the world by advertisement in accord with the rules of court. Subsequently, when the court enters a final adjudication to determine the ownership of the land, such an adjudication is binding on everyone and the individual whose title is adjudicated by the court has good title against the whole world. Another common example of a judgment in rem is the final decree of a court determining the disposition of a decedent's estate.

Acquiring Title by Adverse Possession

Another less common method of acquiring title, but one that deserves attention, is the method of acquiring title, or ownership, by adverse possession. Society has an interest in putting stale claims at rest. The unfortunate consequences of allowing people to present claims many years after their alleged rights came into being is obvious. Witnesses may be nonexistent or else their memories of the events crucial to the claim may be hazy. Honoring such old claims would be an obvious avenue for fraud. Therefore, the legislatures in all of the fifty United States have enacted what are generally called statutes of limitation and are more accurately referred to in law schools as statutes of repose, since they place stale claims at rest permanently.

These statutes of limitation provide that after a certain number of years have elapsed since a right or cause of action arose, one can no longer institute a claim. The periods of time vary in different states and also within a given state, according to the type of action involved. Generally, the time for bringing an action for breach of contract follows the English law and is six years. In the case of torts, such as libel and slander, the period may be much shorter, even as short as one year.

In any event, in the case of a person who has wrongfully taken the property of another and whose use of it has been open, notorious, continuous, and hostile to the rights of the original owner for the period prescribed by the statute of limitations, in the absence of an institution of legal proceedings by the original owner during the prescribed period, the wrongful taker acquires good title and absolute ownership of the property wrongfully taken. The original owner can no longer resort to self-help or avail himself of help from the courts.

However, the requirements as to the nature of the ownership exercised by the wrongful taker during the period in which the statute of limitations is running are strict. He must not have hidden the wrongfully taken property nor used it in a manner consistent with the ownership of the original owner. The use of the property must be continuous for the period prescribed by the statute of limitations. If all the requirements are met, his title is as good as if he purchased the property through a valid agreement of sale. The most common example of adverse possession that the average layman runs into is that involving the use of land.

A home owner, not wishing to create ill will, may allow a neighbor to erect a fence that encroaches several feet on his property. If the encroaching neighbor treats the enclosed land as his own in an open and continuous manner for the period prescribed by the statute of limitations, which, in the case of land, may be 20 years in certain jurisdictions, then he has acquired title to that wrongfully taken land by adverse possession, and his title is as good as if his neighbor who originally owned it had deeded the land to him.

Another example of this type of taking by adverse possession is the case of landowners who have allowed portions of their property to be used as a right of way by the community. If such use persists for 20 years, and is continuous and open, they may find that an easement has been established on their land which is impossible for them to do away with by blocking off the right of way with a fence or other obstruction. The actual period of time required may vary in different jurisdictions.

It may be said that the price of preserving good title to one's real estate is constant vigilance against continuous and open encroachments or trespasses by one's neighbors [12]. Of necessity, our treatment of the complex and important subject of property rights has been extremely superficial at best. However, our intention is to acquaint the reader with the definition of property as a group of rights in objects or in land which are legally recognized and protected by society. Only to the extent that society recognizes and protects the rights of an individual in objects or in land may he be said to own them.

REFERENCES
1. Brown, Ray Andrew. *The law of personal property* (2d Ed.). Chicago: Callaghan & Company, 1936. Pp. 2-3.
2. Brown, pp. 6-7.
3. Brown, pp. 12-13.
4. Brown, pp. 7-10, 15-19.
5. Brown, pp. 23-26.
6. Brown, pp. 28-29.
7. Tiffany, Herbert Thorndike. *The modern law of real property* (New abridged ed. by Carl Zollman). Chicago: Callaghan & Company, 1940. Pp. 736-737.
8. Tiffany, pp. 736-738.
9. Brown, pp. 148-166.
10. Brown, pp. 226-232.
11. Brown, pp. 233-237.
12. Burby, William E. *Handbook of the law of real property* (2d Ed.). St. Paul, Minn.: West Publishing Co., 1954. Chap. 21.

2. INDIVIDUAL RIGHTS

The growth of individual rights throughout the recorded history of mankind parallels the growth of society ruled by law. In truth, an individual can only grow and develop to his maximum potential in a society in which personal freedom is recognized by law; a society in which he may work out his personal destiny within the framework of such laws, free from the whim or caprice of an absolute despot. The growth of this type of individual freedom was slow in coming. We can trace its early beginnings in the history of the English-speaking peoples from whom we derive a great part of our national heritage.

ORIGINS OF ENGLISH LAW
Duke William of Normandy invaded the Saxon kingdom of Britain in 1066, and in that year at the Battle of Hastings established his ascendancy and Norman rule over the British Isles. French influence then became strong in Britain, and French customs and ways were superimposed on the Saxon culture that had prevailed before the invasion. A descendant of William I, Henry II (Henry Plantagenet), came to the throne of England at a time when the powerful barons of the realm were exerting an ever-increasing influence, if not a coercive pressure, on the throne. During his reign, which lasted from 1154 to 1188, Henry Plantagenet affected a dramatic change in the legal system prevailing in Britain, for which many consider him the "father" of British common law.

At the outset of his reign, justice was dispensed by feudal lords to their vassals and others who occupied land under or through them by virtue of the feudal system. Trials by combat were common under the then current theory that the God of Battles would strengthen the arm of the righteous. Perhaps with the idea of giving the God of Battles a little help, many litigants hired professional champions to do their fighting for them at such trials. Other equally bizarre methods of determining the outcome of trials included trial by fire, in which the accused person was asked to hold a hot iron, which, theoretically, would not burn his flesh if he were innocent. Another method of determining the truthfulness of a litigant was to make him eat a morsel of bread, on which, according to the theory of the day, he would choke if he were untruthful. Litigants were sometimes plunged into a pool of water, the thought being that they would not sink if they were telling the truth. Bizarre as these methods may seem to us today, they were the accepted customs of the times.

Henry II attempted, successfully, to offer the people something better and at the same time to draw the court system under the control of the crown. He established royal courts which followed the unique French custom of the jury. The jury was not the impartial panel we know today, but frequently was chosen from among people with first-hand knowledge of the cause to be tried. Individuals were selected who would today be considered witnesses. At the outset of the reign of Henry Plantagenet, the king, and every lord for that matter, had his *peace*, which was another way of saying that offenses committed against him in his presence were punishable by him as crimes. A king's peace extended to offenses committed on his lands and highways. Henry further extended the king's peace to include the entire realm and, by means of a series of writs, drew cases from the feudal courts of the lords into the king's courts. Many litigants, desiring the more impartial brand of justice dispensed by the king's courts, availed themselves of these writs, and by the end of his reign Henry had established a uniform system of laws throughout the British Isles, with the format of trial being basically the same as that which prevails today in the United States and in the British Commonwealth. That is to say, the facts were determined by a jury of 12 men, with the conduct of the trial presided over by a professional judge who instructed the jury in the applicable law.

Of course, the judicial systems promoted by Henry Plantagenet produced the result he sought: namely, strengthening of the king at the expense of the nobles. The royal court system created by Henry II, although a vast improvement over the feudal courts, was not a system completely independent of the control of the sovereign [1].

Elevating the courts to a position coequal with, if not superior to, the crown would have to wait for a later age. The first modest step in that direction took place during the reign of John of Gaunt, the same King John who on June 15, 1215, at the Meadow of Runnymede, signed the Magna Carta. Current history texts have done much to distort the original meaning of the Magna Carta. It was hardly a bill of rights guaranteeing personal freedoms to the ordinary Englishman. The ordinary Englishman was not even considered. When the Magna Carta spoke of "free men," it referred only to the nobility and probably did not descend so far down the scale as to include wealthy merchants.

Many serious students of the Magna Carta feel that it would be better categorized as a bill of privileges than a bill of rights. The barons of the realm, jealous of the various unilateral actions taken by King John, such as raising taxes without their consent, threatened an armed rebellion. Their threats were sufficient to persuade him to sign the Magna Carta, which provides, among other things, that no free man is to be deprived of life, liberty, or property, nor is he to be exiled, except by a judgment of his peers or by the law of the land. The language immediately brings to mind the American Bill of Rights, yet its effect was anything but universal. Another provision of the Magna Carta provided that the king would not raise taxes or take measures important to the kingdom without consulting the barons. This provision clearly put the law above the king and made the king responsible to a body which, if not truly representative, still gave a voice to individuals other than the monarch himself.

The Magna Carta was in fact the forerunner of the present American Bill of Rights, although many struggles and sacrifices in the name of individual freedom were necessary before the rights of the ordinary man were granted the recognition they now receive in the United States and the British Commonwealth.

John Locke, the seventeenth century English philosopher, in his two treatises on government propounded theories of individual rights that were incorporated into the Declaration of Independence by Thomas Jefferson. Locke believed that man had certain inherent rights, and that among these were life, liberty, and the ownership of property. The state existed only to protect the rights of the individual citizens. According to his philosophy, if the state could not offer a citizen better protection for his individual rights than the citizen could provide for himself, then the citizen was justified in finding another ruler. Locke believed in government by the consent of the governed. John Locke died in 1704, but his ideas were immortalized in the Declaration of Independence framed by Thomas Jefferson in 1776.

French Influences

Another spokesman for individual rights during the seventeenth century was the French philosopher Voltaire, who spoke forcefully against government suppression of individual rights and against religious intolerance and persecution. Jean Jacques Rousseau advanced the theory that the only legitimate rulers are those who govern with the consent of the people. He was a strong believer in individual rights and gave great impetus to the French Revolution by his political philosophy. He was a brother in spirit to the English poet, John Milton, who captured the essence of the sixteenth and seventeenth century liberal philosophers by his immortal lines in *Paradise Lost*, "Better to reign in Hell than serve in Heaven."

In this turbulent period of political development among English-speaking peoples, which culminated in the American Revolution, the philosophers, poets, and writers who espoused the cause of individual rights placed their lives, their fortunes, and their honor on the line for their beliefs. Without the dedication and courage they displayed, their wit and brilliance would have been unavailing in the cause of individual freedom.

CIVIL RIGHTS

Civil rights are, in a sense, individual rights with a certain difference. Perhaps the best way to define them collectively is to say that they are rights relating to the basic right not to be discriminated against or singled out for special treatment because of one's race, national origin, religion, sex, or political beliefs.

In the Declaration of Independence, Thomas Jefferson stated that among the self-evident truths is one that holds that "all men are created equal." A cynic later said that, Thomas Jefferson notwithstanding, "some men are created more equal than others." In 1885, in a letter to Joshua Steed, Abraham Lincoln said, "As a nation we began by declaring that all men are created equal. We now practically read it, 'All men are created equal, except Negroes'." In any event, the history of minorities in the United States—whether religious, ethnic, or racial—has been one of discrimination, sometimes subtle and sometimes blatant.

The Struggle for Racial Equality
The opportunities of members of minority groups, such as blacks, Spanish-Americans, Jews, and Orientals, as well as those of Eastern-European descent, to participate fully in and become part of the mainstream of American society, and to enjoy the opportunities derived thereby, have been limited to a greater or lesser degree throughout the history of the United States. Without doubt, those who have suffered most acutely from such discrimination are the blacks. Their situation improved dramatically during the nineteenth century, starting with the Emancipation Proclamation, which was followed by the thirteenth amendment to the Constitution, abolishing slavery in 1865; the fourteenth amendment, making former slaves citizens in 1868; and, in 1870, the fifteenth amendment, prohibiting states from denying citizens the right to vote because of their race and granting all persons under their jurisdiction "equal protection under the laws." However, at the turn of the century, black Americans were still a long way from full participation in the mainstream of American life.

In 1896, the Supreme Court of the United States in the case of *Plessy v. Ferguson* upheld a Louisiana law providing "separate but equal" facilities in railroad cars [2]. For a half century southern states used this decision to justify segregated schools, public accommodations, and recreational facilities. It was only in 1954 that the Supreme Court struck down *Plessy v. Ferguson* in the case of *Brown v. Board of Education of Topeka*, and found segregation in public schools to be unconstitutional inasmuch as it deprived children of equal protection under the law [3]. It further held that separation on the basis of race was never equal. In 1955, the Supreme Court hurried implementation of its decision in the *Brown* case and said that desegregation must be carried out "with all deliberate speed." Finding that the injunction "with all deliberate speed" was not fast enough as it was interpreted by the southern states, the Supreme Court of the United States, in 1969, speeded up the mandate for desegregation by decreeing that it must be carried out "at once."

Toward the middle of the twentieth century, a rising awareness on the part of blacks and other minority groups led to the passage of a number of antidiscrimination bills known as civil rights acts. The Civil Rights Act of 1957, in response to the deliberate delay by southern states in implementing the desegregation order of the Supreme Court, set up a Commission on Civil Rights to investigate violations. It made further provision for implementation by creating the Civil Rights Division of the Department of Justice. Under the Civil Rights Act of 1960, referees were provided to help blacks register to vote. The Civil Rights Act of 1964 prohibited discrimination in public accommodations. It also made it unlawful to discriminate against anyone in employment because of race, color, sex, religion, or national origin, and it provided a commission to implement these provisions. The Civil Rights Act of 1968 outlawed such discrimination in all but a very limited category of real estate rental and sale transactions.

Women's Rights

While the blacks have suffered the most grievously from discrimination in the United States and were the moving force behind much of the civil rights legislation, other minority groups both supported and benefited from the civil rights acts. One group that is not a minority, but has suffered from discrimination in the United States and, in the view of some, throughout the history of mankind, is women.

The first apparent stirrings of discontent among American women came during the woman's suffrage movement. By the middle of the twentieth century, there was a rising awareness among women that the opportunities afforded them by American society did not correspond to their potential for achievement. Feminist leaders pointed out that little girls were trained for traditional feminine roles, in which they would be subservient to men. There were few women in positions of power in business or government. The immediate goal was equal pay for equal work.

With changing morals and a rising divorce rate, many women who found themselves heads of households received substandard pay for doing the same work and accepting the same responsibilities as men. The old argument that a woman really does not need the money as much as a man does is no longer valid, if it ever was.

The Civil Rights Act of 1964, although primarily aimed at alleviating the plight of the blacks, also protected women against discrimination in employment. Corresponding acts were passed by many of the state legislatures, and women began to avail themselves of the rights thus afforded them by filing complaints against discriminating employers. A typical case might involve a group of nurses whose employer discriminated against them unfairly by establishing a lower salary range for nurses than it did for another group of health professionals, the latter being a predominantly male group with very similar educational requirements. A complaint filed with the state Human Relations Commission and the Federal Fair Employment Practices Commission would usually be sufficient to cause revision and equalization of the salary schedules.

Many feminists would classify the nursing profession as one that upholds the traditional feminine roles that they reject for future generations of women, preferring that little girls invade traditional male strongholds, such as the military academies. However, it must be recognized that the nurse's role is changing too.

The American nurse of the 1970s is acting in an ever-expanding role. She is demanding and receiving recognition as a professional and functioning in situations in which her role is anything but passive or submissive. Although men are entering the nursing profession in increasing numbers, it is still a predominantly female profession.

In our opinion, many of the "reforms" sought by leaders of the feminist movement are counterproductive for the majority of American women, an example being a recent erosion in the right of a mother to custody and child support. While no one can argue with a female's right to be free from sex discrimination in pursuing her educational, vocational, and political goals, we think it is questionable whether complete denial of biological differences between men and women in their sexual and parental roles is productive for the well-being of women in our society.

REFERENCES
1. Churchill, Winston S. *The birth of Britain, book two*. New York: Dodd, Mead & Co., 1956. Chap. 13.
2. Plessy v. Ferguson. 163 U.S. 537 (1896).
3. Brown v. Board of Education of Topeka, Shawnee County, Kansas, 74 S. Ct. 686, 347 U.S. 483 (1954).

3. CIVIL LAW
AND COMMON LAW

Two basic legal systems exist in the world today. *Common law*, or law based on prior judicial opinions (sometimes called judge-made law), is the basic system in the United States and most of the British Commonwealth. In the rest of the world, including most European and Latin countries, the basis of the legal system is *civil law*, which consists of law based on codes enacted by legislatures or promulgated as edicts by a sovereign.

THE ROMAN EMPIRE

To have any comprehension of the civil law that applies to one-third of the world, we must examine, at least briefly, the history of the Roman empire, for it is the source of civil law and the philosophy and principles that gave rise to it.

The beginnings of the Roman empire, barely perceptible in outline and shrouded in legend, involve Romulus and Remus, descendants of Aeneas who, according to legend, founded the city of Rome in 735 B.C. Almost 250 years later, in 509 B.C., the Romans rebelled against Tarquinius Superbus, their harsh Etruscan ruler, and declared Rome a republic. The republic was ruled by two consuls elected each year and by the Roman senate. Rome continued as a republic until 27 years after the birth of Christ, when Augustus (Octavian) became the first Roman emperor.

In the year A.D. 395, the Roman empire was divided into an eastern and a western empire. The western empire ended in A.D. 476 when a German chieftan named Odoacer deposed the last Roman emperor of the West, Romulus Augustus. The eastern part of the empire, also known as the Byzantine empire, remained in existence, if barely, until the fall of Constantinople in 1453.

The legal system in effect during the Roman empire was a study in contrast, idealistic in concept, yet harsh and unconscionable in practice because of the weakness, greed, and dishonesty of those who applied it. The basic principles of Roman law have in one degree or other influenced all other legal systems that followed. The first of these principles, and one which applies particularly in civil-law jurisdictions, is that of *single sovereignty*, or the idea that all the laws must emanate from one ruler or ruling body. The second principle is that of universality, or the concept that laws are merely expressions of the needs and requirements of the natural order of society, "natural law." A third concept of Roman law is flexibility, or equity, in which legal remedies are shaped to fit the unique circumstances of a particular case. Even today in our common-law jurisdiction we have a system of equity whereby a chancellor, or judge, is empowered to grant extraordinary relief in unusual cases.

LEGAL HISTORY OF ROMAN EMPIRE

In terms of legal history, the period from the founding of the city of Rome in 753 B.C. to the establishment of the Roman republic has been called by some historians the period of conjecture. Little accurate information exists about the legal institutions and the laws during this era. They may be recreated only on the basis of inferences derived from later institutions and from tradition and legend.

In the year 450 B.C., approximately 60 years after the founding of the republic, the plebeian class (common people) wrested a concession from the Roman government. Previously the law had been largely unwritten and was subject to molding and modification by upper class or patrician magistrates who administered it to the detriment of plebeian litigants. As a concession to plebeian grievances in regard to this practice, the government enacted the Twelve Tables, which codified the basic Roman laws. Many copies of these tables were made and they were considered so important that Cicero speaks of boys of his time being required to learn them by heart. Surprisingly, however, no complete copy of the Twelve Tables has survived the ravages of time. We may deduce the contents of the tables only by inference and from the few existing fragments.

A great deal of Roman legal history was lost in the burning and sacking of Rome by the Gauls in 387 B.C. Few accurate records exist prior to this date. During the latter part of Rome's history as a republic, from the second century B.C. to the founding of the empire in 27 B.C., Roman law was divided into two major categories. They were the *ius honorarium*, which was law derived from edicts of the magistrates and which applied only to Roman citizens, and the *ius gentium*, which was the law applied by Roman magistrates to foreigners and Roman subjects who were not citizens.

The difference between these two legal systems was distinct at first, with the ius gentium being based on the law of the merchants who held sway in the Mediterranean port cities. Over the years the differences became indistinct since both the ius honorarium and the ius gentium were supposedly based on natural law, common to all mankind. Roman law was also divided into *ius scriptum*, which was written law, and *ius non scriptum*, unwritten law. The Romans gave great weight to unwritten law, which was in many cases merely custom. According to the then current theory, custom showed what Romans wished the law to be. In many cases the custom was later codified and became ius scriptum.

The Roman ideal was universality, with all law emanating from one source. In fact, Roman law emanated from many sources. Plebeian assemblies, or *plebiscita*, enacted laws that were of great importance. The senate passed resolutions known as *consulta senatatis*, which were also given the force of law. Unlike the plebiscita, the senate was composed of upper-class individuals known as patricians. Perhaps the greatest and most important sources of law were known as *edicta magistrata*, edicts passed by the magistrates. During the early history of Rome and after the founding of the republic (until 367 B.C.), the king or counsel decided important legal cases. The growth of business and litigation finally made this impossible and in 367 B.C. a magistrate, or *praetor*, was appointed for the purpose of trying cases. The praetors had wide law-making powers and they formulated laws by means of edicts set at the beginning of their terms of office. The total body of these edicts was known as the edicta magistrata and was, as we have previously noted, also subdivided into the law applying to Romans, the ius honorarium, and the law applying to foreigners, the ius gentium.

Praetors held office for a one-year term, at the beginning of which they would issue an edict that would define the law in their jurisdiction for the coming year. Customarily, the praetors would reissue the edict of their predecessor in office with few changes. Praetors were generally members of the patrician class and were frequently appointed to the senate after their term in office had expired. The lower class, or plebeians, resented the wide authority of the praetors to make and change laws to suit their own purposes. As a result of this, in 131 B.C., the emperor Hadrian ordered the praetor, Savius Iulianus, to revise and settle the praetorian edicts, which thereafter could only be amended by the emperor.

The legal profession, as we know it today, probably had its beginnings in the Roman empire. For about 600 years, from 304 B.C. to A.D. 300, a class of men schooled in the law, and known as *prudentes*, exercised a great influence on Roman law since their *responsa* (opinions) were given great weight by the magistrates and praetors who decided cases. Frequently, the magistrate was not an expert in the law and relied heavily on the opinions of the lawyers involved in the case. These lawyers did not engage in the practice of law as a livelihood nor did they give opinions for a fee. They were generally members of the patrician or upper class, and were often men with political ambitions. Their opinions were given without charge, yet we may surmise that many indirect benefits accrued to them as a result of their professional status.

To the Roman ideal of universality in the law, the emperor Justinian made his greatest contribution. He, along with his chief minister, Tribonian, was responsible for codifying the vast body of Roman law into three great works. They were the digests that contained the best opinions of Roman jurists, eliminating extraneous material and conflicting opinions while retaining that which was best.

Another major work initiated by Justinian that influenced the education of lawyers for centuries was the *Institutes* of A.D. 533. These were standard texts created for the law schools at the universities of Berytus (Beirut) and Constantinople (Istanbul). Justinian's Code of A.D. 534, a collection of imperial constitutions, became an important reference for the study of Roman law for the following centuries.

In an explanation of the origin of Roman law, a brief reference should be made to how the law regarded people. All men were divided into two categories, free men and slaves. A slave was a chattel at the mercy of his master and without rights or duties except for a duty to obey the criminal laws. Free men were divided into three classes: the patrician or upper class, the *equites* who were primarily rich merchants, and the plebeians. Originally, Roman citizenship was not extended to all free men; however, the privilege of citizenship was gradually extended to Roman subjects throughout the empire other than slaves.

Roman law provided that the male head of a family, the *paterfamilias*, had extreme authority. Originally, a father could even inflict capital punishment on his children and male lineal descendants, and he had absolute rights over their property and earnings. In the latter stages of the Roman empire, however, these rights were severely limited. Roman marriages were in many respects similar to our civil or even common-law marriages today. They were nonreligious and nonceremonial. Divorce by a simple act of repudiation was available to either party. In most cases, each party could own separate property and a wife could recover her dowry if the marriage ended by either divorce or the husband's death. Later in the history of the Roman empire, Christian emperors imposed penalties on those who divorced without good reason, but the freedom to divorce was not taken away. Unlike the common-law systems, Roman law made little or no distinction between real estate and personal property.

Many European countries adopted codes that were mere modifications of Justinian's works. Some of the most noteworthy examples were the Napoleonic Code adopted by France in 1804, the Austrian Code of 1811, the Swiss Civil Code of 1912, and the Greek Code of 1946. Countries under civil law comprise more than one-third of the world and, in spite of differing economic, social, political, and historical backgrounds, their legal structures function effectively on the basic framework set forth in Justinian's Code.

DEVELOPMENT OF ENGLISH COMMON LAW

It may reasonably be said that the common-law system that prevails in the United States and the British Commonwealth today is an outgrowth of the civil law brought to Britain by the Romans. Henry II, who reigned in England from 1154 to 1188, was anxious to draw the control of the courts away from independent and sometimes rebellious lords. As mentioned previously, he established the "king's peace," which was a universal law throughout the realm administered by judges appointed by the king. In their search for uniformity, the king's justices, riding circuit, looked to each other's decisions as precedents in similar cases, and the principle of *stare decisis*, or law based on prior judicial decisions, was born.

The first general and comprehensive statement of English law as it was developing through judicial opinion was written by a chief justice of England, one Henry of Bracton, in 1250. It was called "A Tract on the Laws and Customs of England," and it represented a major step forward in the development of our present system of common law [1]. Although it would seem that Henry Plantagenet is most deserving of the title "father of the common law," no commentary on that legal system, however brief, would be complete without mentioning Sir Edward Coke, without a doubt the greatest common lawyer of all time. This eminent Englishman was born in Norfolk in 1552 to a family of lawyers. His distinguished career in public life began with service as attorney general to Queen Elizabeth I in 1594. He acted as prosecutor at many famous treason trials and was better known for his zeal in obtaining convictions than for his concern for the rights of the defendants.

In 1607, at the age of 54, Coke became chief justice of the court of common pleas under James I. It was at this point that his personality and philosophy underwent a dramatic change. During the ensuing years, on many occasions he risked his life and fortune by successfully asserting the supremacy of the common law, as administered by judges, over the king's prerogative. By the time of Coke's death in 1634, he had lost his position as chief justice of England, but he had successfully established the supremacy of the common-law courts and the rule of law [2].

Over the years that have ensued since the reign of Henry II, the distinctions between common law and civil law have become more difficult to define. Certainly it is no longer accurate to say that civil law is derived from codes or edicts enacted by the sovereign or the legislature, whereas common law may be derived exclusively from the decisions of judges. Much of what passes as common law has been reduced to codes and much civil law is found in the writings of legal scholars and in custom.

CIVIL LAW AND COMMON LAW TODAY

Reginald Parker, an eminent legal scholar, has distinguished the two systems as they exist today on the basis of their underlying philosophy. According to Parker, one basic distinction between common law and civil law is that civil lawyers are trained to reason deductively and common lawyers are trained to reason inductively. For example a civil lawyer, reasoning deductively, will say that all men must die, F is a man, therefore F must die. A common lawyer might say that, based on his observation, A,

B, C, D, and E are men and they have died. He will therefore induce that F, a man, will die. In other words, civil law is based on reasoning to specific conclusions from unquestioned general basic premises, while common law is founded on inductive reasoning based on observation and experience.

Another basic difference between common-law jurisdictions and civil-law jurisdictions is that a rule of stare decisis is renounced in civil-law jurisdiction, and a judge's decision in a specific case does not have general application to other similar cases. In a common-law jurisdiction, a judge's decision on a particular set of facts is a precedent in similar cases until it is overruled.

A third basic distinction between the philosophy of the civil law and that of the common law is that rather than rely on prior judicial decisions, civil lawyers and courts rely on learned writers and legal scholars in the tradition of the Roman lawyers or prudentes, whose opinions had the force of law [3].

While our discussion of the comparison of civil and common law may seem to have little direct application to the field of nursing, no true understanding of the laws under which we live can be had without the ability to distinguish between these two systems.

REFERENCES
1. Churchill, Winston S. *The birth of Britain, book two.* New York: Dodd, Mead, 1956. Chap. 13.
2. Bowen, Catherine Drinker. *The lion and the throne—The life and times of Sir Edward Coke.* Boston: Little, Brown, 1957.
3. Parker, Reginald. The criteria of the civil law. *The Jurist* 7:141, 1947.

4. AMERICAN GOVERNMENT

THE COURT SYSTEM

In the United States the Federal Constitution is the highest law of the land. It establishes the basic framework of our government. Under the Constitution the federal government is a government of reserved powers; that is, all powers not reserved to the federal government are granted to the individual states. We have two court systems in the United States, the *federal system* and the *state court system*. The federal court system has jurisdiction over a very limited category of cases that are reserved to it as part of the judicial power granted the federal government by the United States Constitution. The federal court system retains jurisdiction over cases involving consuls, ambassadors, treaties, controversies between an individual and the state or between the different states, violations of federal statutes, and controversies involving the constitutionality of state and federal statutes.

Article III, section 1 of the Federal Constitution provides the following:

The judicial Power of the United States, shall be vested in one supreme Court, and in such inferior Courts as the Congress may from time to time ordain and establish. The Judges, both of the supreme and inferior Courts, shall hold their Offices during good Behaviour, and shall, at stated Times, receive for their Services, a Compensation, which shall not be diminished during their Continuance in Office.

Under the authority of article III, section 1 of the Constitution, Congress has provided by statute that there shall be a Supreme Court consisting of eight associate judges and one chief justice. Actual trials in the federal system are held in the federal district courts, of which there are 93. The United States is divided into 11 circuits, each of which has its own court of appeals. Appeals from a federal district court within a given circuit are taken to the circuit court of appeals. The court of appeals is for most purposes the court of last resort of the federal system, since the United States Supreme Court hears appeals from the court of appeals only at its own discretion by granting a *writ of certiorari*. Under certain circumstances the Supreme Court may also hear appeals directly from the highest court of the given state, for example, the Supreme Court of Pennsylvania.

Various other more specialized courts exist in the federal system, such as the admiralty courts, which deal with maritime problems, the tax claim court, the court of customs and patent appeals, and the military court system [1].

The state courts may exercise all the powers not reserved to the federal courts by the Constitution and, in many cases, have powers concurrent with those of the federal court system. In the state system, the lowest state courts are generally referred to as magistrates' courts and consist of courts of very limited jurisdiction over criminal and civil matters. They are presided over by one individual, usually referred to as a magistrate or justice of the peace. These individuals are collectively referred to as the minor judiciary and are frequently not lawyers. Verbatim transcripts are not required to be kept in the proceedings of these courts and, therefore, they are also frequently called courts not of record. Under certain circumstances, at the option of one or both of the parties involved in a case, a court reporter may make a verbatim transcript of proceedings in the court of a magistrate or justice of the peace.

The next level of court in the state system is the trial court of general jurisdiction, frequently referred to as a court of common pleas. These courts can award money damages and equitable relief without limitation in civil cases within their jurisdiction, and can impose any authorized punishment in criminal matters.

All states have an appellate court of last resort, frequently known as the supreme court or court of appeals, and most of the states have an intermediate appellate court as well.

Perhaps the best way for a lay person to gain some comprehension of the various court systems in the United States is to follow the progress of a hypothetical case through court.

Our story starts with our central character, Pamela Painful, a 47-year-old housewife and mother of three, who resided in New Jersey with her husband and family. Because she had severe coronary problems, she was under the care of a cardiologist on the staff of Albatross General Hospital, also located in New Jersey. On the advice of her cardiologist, she consulted Florence Scalpel, M.D., a surgeon also on the staff at Albatross, and was finally admitted to that hospital for open-heart surgery. Immediately after Pamela Painful left the operating room following her open-heart surgert, she was transferred to the intensive care unit (ICU), arriving there at 4:00 P.M. Dr. Scalpel had marked her chart "vital signs and dressing Q 15 minutes." Helen Heedless, R.N., the head nurse of the unit, had her usual staff of three registered nurses on duty in the ICU at the time Pamela was admitted. One of them was leaving the hospital to get married at the end of her shift. At 5:00 P.M., Heedless told all three of her assistants that they could go to the cafeteria for a little farewell get-together with some of the other nurses, and that she was quite able to manage Pamela Painful and Mr. Heartblock, the only two patients then in the ICU.

Immediately after the three assistants left, things started to happen. Mr. Heartblock had a cardiac arrest and required Heedless' undivided attention for approximately 45 minutes. By the time Heartblock's vital signs had stabilized, another patient had been admitted from the operating room, and before Heedless had a chance to check Pamela again it was 6:15 P.M.. Heedless found her comatose, with her dressing soaked with blood. She called the resident immediately. Although Pamela ultimately responded to treatment and regained consciousness, she had suffered brain damage that resulted in permanent blindness. When she left the hospital, she consulted Henry Tort, Esq., her family lawyer, about her legal rights.

Tort suggested that she had a claim against Heedless, the resident, and the hospital. He agreed to represent her on a contingent fee basis whereby he would receive one-third of any recovery. Tort immediately wrote to Heedless, the hospital, and the resident to inform them of his representation of Pamela. After unsuccessfully attempting to negotiate a fair settlement with the various insurance companies involved, Tort informed Pamela that an adequate recovery could be made only by starting suit. Pamela authorized Tort to proceed in the manner he thought best.

A case such as that which Pamela Painful wishes to bring may be started in federal court under two circumstances: one circumstance is that in which there is a substantial federal question involving the constitutionality of a state or federal law, or in which there is a special provision that Congress has made for suit in a federal district court; the other cimcumstance is that involving diversity of citizenship. In a case in which the plaintiff and the defendant are citizens of different states and in which the amount in controversy is in excess of $10,000, suit may be brought in the federal district court.

Tort realized that because the plaintiff and the defendants were citizens of different states (Heedless had moved to Pennsylvania) and the damages could reasonably be claimed to be in excess of $10,000, he had the right to bring suit in the Federal District Court of Pennsylvania or in that of New Jersey. He could also bring suit in the state courts, but was required to make a choice. Experience in trial work led Tort to believe that his chance for a large verdict was greater in the federal district court where the juries represent more of a cross section of the population and are chosen from a wider geographical area than in the state courts. Federal juries are generally more educated and sophisticated than state court juries and better able to understand complicated cases and the need for large awards. Furthermore, federal judges exercise closer control of the progress of the case toward trial. There is less delay in a case being reached for trial, and federal courts tend to be very intolerant of lateness or dilatory tactics on the part of attorneys.

Tort also knew that in the federal court system a case would be tried under the law of New Jersey, where the cause of action arose, even though he had a choice of starting suit in the federal district court of either New Jersey or Pennsylvania [2]. For his convenience and that of his client, he chose to institute suit in a federal district court in New Jersey. An added consideration was the inconvenience this choice would cause Heedless, who lived in Pennsylvania. Such an added burden on his opponent, Tort speculated, might facilitate a settlement. Tort prepared a complaint, or a statement of the facts on which Pamela based her claim for damages, and filed it with the clerk of the federal district court in Camden, New Jersey.

A copy of the complaint was served on Heedless by a United States Marshall, and she in turn took the complaint to her malpractice insurance carrier, who referred the matter to its attorney, Mr. Blackstone. Blackstone realized that if he did not file an answer within twenty days, a default judgment could be entered against Heedless. Heedless, being something of a perfectionist, was unwilling to admit to herself that she had done anything wrong. She told Blackstone that she had never given her assistants permission to leave and that they had done so against her orders. Blackstone set forth Heedless' version of the incident in a written statement of defense, called an answer, which he filed with the clerk of the district court, and he sent a copy to Tort. At this point the factual controversy between the parties was clear and the case was "at issue."

Within a short period, probably sixty days after suit has been started, the federal judge to whom the case has been assigned holds a preliminary conference in his chambers, at which time he set dates for the following stages of progress of the case: the completion of pre-trial discovery, filing of a pre-trial memorandum by attorneys for both parties, a pre-trial conference, and the actual date of trial.

Discovery proceedings in federal and state courts are very similar and the purpose is the same. They are designed to narrow the issues of fact to be decided by the jury at the trial and to enable each side to discover the facts necessary to properly prepare its case. Various methods are commonly used for pre-trial discovery. Perhaps the most common is the oral deposition, whereby a witness is questioned by one party or the other, and the questions and answers are recorded by a court reporter, whose transcript is made a part of the record of the case and may under certain circumstances be introduced as evidence at the trial.

Each side may file written *interrogatories* and serve them on the other party. Interrogatories are questions which, under federal procedure, must be answered in writing and under oath within thirty days of the time they are served. Any questions and answers also become part of the record of the case and may be used in a manner similar to the transcript of oral depositions. Parties may also serve lists of facts on the opposing side which must be admitted or denied in writing within thirty days of the time the requests for admission are served. Any fact thus submitted must be considered established for the purpose of trial and need not be otherwise proved to the jury.

The pre-trial memorandum, which the attorneys must file at the conclusion of discovery proceedings, sets forth all the facts which have been proved or admitted in the discovery proceedings, lists the facts which each side hopes to prove at the trial, and enumerates the principles of law on which each side is relying.

Once discovery has been completed and the pre-trial memorandum has been prepared, a case is generally 95 percent ready for trial. At the pre-trial conference the trial judge attempts to narrow the issues of fact which the jury must decide by getting the attorneys to agree to certain facts on the genuineness of relative documents as to which there is no real controversy. The trial judge also attempts to persuade the attorneys to settle their case amicably before the trial. Experience has shown that the period immediately before trial, starting with the pre-trial conference, is a period in which the vast majority of cases are settled.

If no settlement is reached, the judge issues a pre-trial order, which covers the stipulations reached at the pre-trial conference and sets forth the issues of fact remaining for determination by a jury. Both attorneys must sign the pre-trial order and, except in unusual cases, it will control the conduct of the trial.

Tort felt that he needed to know more about Heedless' defense before trial and arranged to have the three assistants who had left the ICU subpoenaed, so that they could be questioned before a court reporter and their answers recorded. The results were conflicting. One of the assistants said she had left without permission, but the other two were very emphatic in declaring they had had permission from Heedless before they went.

Mr. Tort, Pamela's lawyer, shared the attitude of most trial lawyers that a jury trial is the final resort when all attempts at a reasonable settlement have been exhausted. Trials are uncertain in their outcome and expensive for the parties, especially where bodily injuries are involved. Physicians who act as expert witnesses charge substantial fees, sometimes as much as $1500 a day for testimony in court. Other witnesses must be paid as well, and it is not unusual in a case involving serious bodily injury for the costs of trial to exceed $10,000.

When they considered all of this, Pamela and her lawyer still felt they had no recourse but to proceed to trial. Since Tort was unsuccessful in settling Pamela's claim before trial, he was then required to appear with Pamela and her witnesses, whose presence might be required by subpoena if they would not appear voluntarily, and any objects or documents he wished to introduce as evidence at the federal district court house at the time and date designated by the judge in his pre-trial order.

Unless a jury has been waived by the parties and the judge designated as a trier of fact, the first order of business is selecting a jury. The trial is started by the selection by both attorneys of a jury of twelve men and women from a panel. Once a jury has been selected, counsels for both sides make opening arguments in which they outline their case and set forth to the jury the facts that have been admitted prior to trial and the facts that they intend to prove by the introduction of evidence.

In a jury trial, the judge acts as a referee in the sense that he sees to it that the evidence is presented in an orderly manner and in accord with federal rules of civil procedure. He rules on objections to the evidence and insists on order and decorum in the courtroom. At the close of the evidence, when both sides have rested their cases, the attorneys have an opportunity to make closing arguments to the jury, in which they recapitulate the theory of their case, review the evidence they have presented, and point out the weaknesses in their opponent's case. The judge then instructs the jury on the legal principles they must apply to the facts in finding a verdict. The judge is the final authority on the law and the jury is the final authority on the facts. They apply the facts to the law, as presented by the judge, and attempt to reach a just verdict that will fairly compensate the plaintiff if, in fact, they find that any compensation is due.

At the trial of the case the jury awarded Pamela $150,000 in damages. Blackstone decided to take an appeal, since he felt the judge who presided at the trial allowed Tort to ask Pamela leading questions and had, in addition, improperly instructed the jury regarding the law before they began their deliberations. Blackstone filed a motion for a new trial and argued this motion before the judge who presided at the trial. When Blackstone's motion for a new trial was refused, he appealed to the circuit court of appeals. As part of his appeal, a complete record of the testimony, the evidence, and the judge's instructions was presented to the court of appeals. The court of appeals heard no new evidence, merely making a judgment on the record regarding whether Blackstone's client, Heedless, had received a fair trial at the district court in Camden. Both attorneys had an opportunity to make an oral argument and present written briefs in support of their respective positions before the court of appeals. The court, ruling in favor of the appellee, Pamela Painful, held that the order of the district court refusing a new trial had been proper and that there had been no prejudicial error in the conduct of the trial or in the instructions to the jury. The judgment of the district court was, therefore, affirmed.

At this point, Heedless and Tort had reached what in most cases is considered "the end of the line" in federal civil proceedings. There is no absolute right of appeal from the court of appeals to the United States Supreme Court. Appeals to the Supreme Court are allowed at its discretion, and it may issue a *writ of certiorari* (an order that brings into a higher court for review the record of the proceedings of a lower court) to the court of appeals when it decides to hear an appeal. Blackstone realized that there was nothing of national importance about his case that would influence the Supreme Court to grant him the right to appeal it and he regretfully informed the insurance carrier for Heedless that it would have to pay the award as well as all the court costs including interest.

Our story could have had a different ending. In any event, the reader will see that to establish one's rights by litigation may be a slow and costly process in which the outcome is far from certain. Many people have made suggestions for speeding up the judicial process, but most of the suggestions involve removing some of the safeguards that ensure fairness to all parties.

LEGISLATION
Organization of the Legislature

Many of the laws that prevail in the United States originate from the statutes enacted by the United States Congress and the legislatures of the individual states. The United States Congress and the state legislatures have similar structures. Anyone who has an understanding of the course of a bill through the Congress to the point where it becomes a law of the land will have no trouble in comprehending the same process in the state legislature. The United States Congress is a *bicameral* legislative body; that is, it is composed of two houses, an "upper house," or the Senate, and a "lower house," or the House of Representatives.

The Senate is composed of 100 members, two from each of the 50 states. These members are elected for a term of six years. At the time senators are elected, they must be at least 30 years old and must have been a citizen of the United States for nine years and a resident of the state in which they are elected. Continuity is provided by a system in which one-third of the members of the Senate are elected every two years. The elections are also arranged so that the terms of two senators from one state do not expire at the same time.

The House of Representatives of the Congress is composed of 435 members elected every two years from among the 50 states and apportioned according to population. The correct designation of members of the lower house is "representative in Congress"; however, they are popularly known as congressmen. The Constitution provides that there shall be no more than one congressman for every 300,000 of population. The Supreme Court ruled that "As nearly as is practical one man's vote in a congressional election is to be worth as much as another's." This principle was set forth in the Supreme Court's opinion in the case of *Kirkpatrick v. Preisler* and is commonly referred to as the "one man, one vote" principle. The decision attempted to rectify the situation in the United States whereby the constituents of a congressman elected from a district with 30,000 voters had a much greater voice than those of a congressman elected from a district having 175,000 voters. A representative must be at least 25 years old and must have been a citizen for 7 years and a resident of the state from which chosen at the time of election.

Legislative Powers of Congress

The Constitution provides that all bills involving expenditures or taxes must originate in the House of Representatives. A representative in Congress must stand for election every two years. By creating such a short term for representatives, the framers of the Constitution obviously intended to provide for a lower house that was extremely responsive to the will of the people. It has been said by students of the United States

Congress that congressmen start running for election the moment they take office. This is not far from the truth in the case of representatives who want to be sure of reelection. The writers of the Constitution, knowing that taxation and the appropriation of monies constitute one of the most sensitive areas for which Congress is responsible, provided that all such legislation must originate in the House of Representatives, the more responsive of the two houses of Congress.

On the other hand, in an attempt to provide a counter-balance to a volatile Congress, the framers of the Constitution provided for a senate, in which the members are insulated from the pressures of election for six years. The Senate, too, has unique powers. Under the Constitution it has the exclusive right to give final approval to treaties with foreign nations and certain nominations for important office by the president. Although the salaries of senators and congressmen are the same, the fact that there are only two senators from each state gives each senator a much greater constituency than a representative and that, combined with the longer term, gives senators a higher status than representatives in Congress. The Senate has been referred to as "the most exclusive club in the world," and many regard the office of senator as second only to that of President of the United States.

IMPEACHMENT. In regard to impeachment of the president or other higher federal officers, the Constitution provides for a division of duties between the Senate and the House of Representatives. The charges in the impeachment proceedings are brought in the House of Representatives, which functions in much the same manner as a grand jury. If it finds a *prima facie* case, or grounds for a trial, instead of indicting in the manner of a grand jury, it finds *articles of impeachment*. The actual trial on the articles of impeachment is then held in the Senate with the Chief Justice of the United States presiding. This whole procedure might have seemed rather academic to most Americans until the Watergate scandal, which dramatized the first half of the process, at least, on millions of television screens throughout the nation.

Sources of Legislation

The ideas that are eventually acted on in the form of bills come to Congress from three basic sources. The representatives and senators themselves, of course, observe problems in their states or legislative districts that they feel could be solved by appropriate legislation. Sometimes they feel that laws already in effect do not answer the needs of the people and need to be repealed or amended. Of course the constituents who elect the representatives and senators have ideas of their own, and the senators and the representatives, who wish to be reelected, know that they must listen sympathetically to these ideas and translate them, if they have merit, into laws. Executive communications are another source of ideas and suggestions for laws that are extremely important to both senators and congressmen. An executive communication is usually in the form of a letter from a member of the president's cabinet, from the president himself, or in some cases, from an independent agency such as the Defense Department or the Treasury Department. Under section 3 of article II of the Constitution, the president has an obligation to report to Congress from time to time on the state of the union and to make recommendations for laws that he deems necessary and expedient. Many of the executive messages are delivered to Congress following the president's state of the union message and they carry in more specific terms the recommendations made by the president in his report to Congress.

Bills into Law

There are two basic ways in which a proposed law may be introduced to Congress. A bill may be introduced in either house by filing the proposed law with the Speaker of the House of Representatives or the president of the Senate. For the purposes of this chapter, we will consider a bill starting in the House of Representatives. The proposed bill must be signed by at least one of its sponsoring members. It is then placed in a box known as the "hopper" at the side of the clerk's desk. The bill is then referred to an appropriate committee by the Speaker of the House. Under the terms of the Legislative Reorganization Act of 1946, there are now 21 standing committees in the House of Representatives and 17 in the Senate.

The procedure for referring a bill to committee in the Senate is similar to that in the House of Representatives, but slightly more formal. Once the bill has been received by the appropriate committee, the public is given notice by an entry in the *Congressional Record* and often in newspapers and periodicals. The committee may then hold public hearings on the bill; these are often covered by television and radio in the case of legislation of great public interest. These hearings are often held through a subcommittee of the standing committee. The bill may then be reported by the subcommittee to the full committee, either favorably or unfavorably and with or without amendments. If the subcommittee has not taken a favorable view of the proposed bill, it most frequently suggests that it be tabled or taken out of consideration indefinitely. The standing committee then considers the bill and either tables it, which to all intents and purposes terminates the proposed legislation, or reports on it favorably or unfavorably to the full House. Once a bill is reported on by a committee to the full House, it is placed on a calendar and is considered in turn, except in the case of legislation for which there is an immediate need. In that case, there are special provisions for considering such bills out of turn.

Once a bill has been passed by the House of Representatives, it is sent to the Senate, where it is also referred to committee and ultimately considered by the entire upper house. If it is passed by the Senate in a different form than that in which it was passed by the House, a conference committee of senators and representatives is appointed to work out the differences. When a compromise has been reached, the bill is brought back to both houses for ratification.

In order for a bill to be presented to the President for approval, it must be passed in identical form by both houses of Congress. When this has been done, the final copy of the bill, with all the amendments added, is called the enrolled bill and must be signed by the Speaker of the House and the president of the Senate before being presented to the President of the United States. Once the President signs the bill, it becomes law. He may, however, reject the bill, or veto it, and send it back to Congress with his reasons for the rejection. In this case, a two-thirds vote by both houses of Congress in favor of the bill will override the President's veto. A bill may also become a law by failure of the President to return it with his reasons for rejection within ten days of the time he receives it, while Congress is in session.

Historically, the United States Senate is known for its lengthy debates. A tactic frequently used by senators representing a minority point of view, who wish to delay legislation they consider unfavorable, is the *filibuster*. This is the method whereby senators representing such a minority point of view engage in lengthy speeches so as to delay consideration of all other important legislation. At the present time, there is a provision for cutting off such debate if 16 senators sign a motion for *cloture* and the motion is carried by two-thirds of the members of the Senate present and voting.

Legislation and the Nurse
As we can see from the previous discussion, legislation affecting nurses will be derived from many sources. It may originate from the suggestions of such professional nursing groups as the American Nurses' Association, which suggests what it considers to be needed legislation to representatives in Congress or to senators it regards as sympathetic to the needs of the nursing profession. New legislation may also originate in the form of executive communications from the Department of Health, Education, and Welfare or other departments of the executive branch. It may also originate with individual nurses who contact their senators or representatives in Congress and express their views in regard to the need for new legislation or the amendment of existing legislation.

From whatever source these ideas come, they must be put in the form of a written bill and go through the committee process. If they relate to the health field, they will most likely be considered by the Subcommittee on Health of the Senate Finance Committee and the Subcommittee on Health of the House Ways and Means Committee. Although a bill may be tabled at any stage of the proceedings, if it is destined for passage it will be reported favorably by the subcommittee to the standing committee, which will then report the bill favorably to the entire house of which it is a part.

The procedures in the various state legislatures closely parallel those in the United States Congress. The two-house system is similar, with an upper house elected for a longer term and a lower house with a larger membership and a shorter term of office than the upper house. The committee system is also followed and the sources of ideas for bills are much the same as on the federal level, with ideas coming from the governor and various executive branches of the state government as well as from concerned citizens and groups [1].

It is apparent that the evolving role of the professional nurse is closely tied to the passage of appropriate legislation. The nurse practice acts in various states define the role of the nurse, and the appropriation bills passed by the United States Congress and the state legislatures support nursing education. Nurses must acquaint themselves with the legislative process and make sure there is a continual input of ideas to keep the law-making bodies informed of the needs of the nursing profession in terms of appropriate legislation. Nurses must also monitor, through their professional associations, legislation introduced in Congress and in state legislatures that would adversely affect the nursing profession. Legislative liaison personnel and lobbyists play a vital and important role in representing the interests of the nursing profession to the legislatures.

In short, what a nurse is allowed to do and prohibited from doing, what her legal rights and liabilities are, and what she must pay for her education are all to a great degree determined by legislation. This is a field in which the nurse has an obligation to herself and to her profession to keep herself well informed.

REFERENCES

1. *Our American government.* House Document No. 93-153. Washington, D.C.: U.S. Government Printing Office, 1973.
2. Moore, James William; Vestal, Allan D.; and Kurland, Phillip B. *Moore's manual: Federal practice and procedure.* New York: Matthew Bender, 1975. Vol. 1, chap. 4.

5. TORTS

CRIMES, TORTS, AND HYBRIDS

Certain offenses against persons or property are so grave in their consequences to society in general that the individual who perpetrates them is punished by a fine, imprisonment, or even death. These offenses are known as crimes. The punishment is not related to compensating the victim for his loss, but is rather directed toward deterring others from committing similar offenses. Examples of offenses almost universally punished as crimes are robbery, rape, and murder.

Another group of offenses against persons and property in which society does not have as great an interest as it does in crimes are known as torts. This category does not include breach of contract, but does include such varied offenses as libel, slander, professional malpractice, assault and battery, and false imprisonment. While some torts may also be crimes, in general, torts are acts that are noncriminal and are not punished by sanctions such as fine and imprisonment.

In the case of a tort, the person or party injured by the offense may sue the offender in a civil action for compensation by money damages. It is safe to say that most crimes are fairly apparent to any civilized person who knows "the difference between right and wrong." Torts, on the other hand, are more complex in their characteristics and subtle in their variations. They are frequently difficult to define. The torts which are easiest for a lay person to understand are intentional torts, such as assault and battery, trespass on real estate, and defamation of character. These are not the torts that are of most concern to a professional nurse.

TORTS AND THE NURSE

The nursing profession in recent years has developed an interest almost bordering on paranoia in the type of unintentional tort that is based on negligence, or failure to carry out a duty of care and professional competence owed to a patient. Torts of this type may be generally classified as those involving professional malpractice.

Nursing educators expend a great deal of effort in informing their students of the measures they must take and the pitfalls they must avoid in order to protect themselves from suit. We feel that much of the emphasis on this type of instruction is wrong. While it is important for professional nurses to have an overview of the law and a general understanding of their legal rights and liabilities, these will not prevent them from being sued. The best way for a nurse to avoid being sued is to deliver good health care. Next to good health care delivery, rapport between the nurse and her patient ranks a close second in preventing actions for malpractice. Of course, much of this rapport is a function of a nurse's personality and cannot be taught at a school of nursing. The health professional who presents himself or herself to a patient as coldly omniscient and unapproachable had better beware of unsatisfactory results. With such unsympathetic treatment, a patient's disappointment can quickly turn to rage and hostility, which may be vented in a lawsuit whether or not the unsatisfactory result was caused by negligence.

In general, it may be said that the law imposes an obligation on everyone to use a reasonable degree of care in carrying out his or her affairs, so that they will not harm other persons or the property of others. Reasonable care is that degree of care which a reasonable, prudent person would use under the circumstances [1]. This standard is affected by the age, sex, experience, education, and skill of the individual involved, so that in determining the reasonable person against whose hypothetical conduct a nurse's conduct would be measured, we might in fact superimpose on this model the nurse's own characteristics. We might ask, for example, what degree of care would a reasonably prudent 32-year-old female registered nurse who holds a B.S.N. degree use under the circumstances. In the case of professionals, nurses and others who hold themselves out to the public as having special skills, there is a duty to use that degree of skill prevalent among their peers. In other words, a professional nurse has a duty, in caring for her patients, to use the degree of skill that is prevalent in her community among nurses of similar education and experience. For example, let us assume that Nurse Jones is 32 years old, holds a B.S.N. degree, and has had 10 years of experience. She is employed in a general hospital in city X. She would be negligent if she failed to use either the degree of care or skill prevalent among nurses of equivalent background in city X. If, as a result of such negligence, one of her patients was injured, the patient would have the right to sue Nurse Jones for money damages. Since it is often difficult to obtain the testimony of a nurse regarding the prevailing standard of care in her community when the suit involves a claim against one of her colleagues, some jurisdictions allow the standard of care and skill imposed on a nurse to be that prevailing in a "similar locality," thereby allowing the testimony of a nurse from another, similar community to be admitted.

NURSE PRACTICE ACTS

Many states have enacted legislation expanding the role of professional nurses. These acts are generally referred to as *nurse practice acts*. One of the most sensitive areas in which the nursing profession has been given an expanded role under the new legislation is diagnosis. Under the Professional Nursing Law of Pennsylvania, nurses are given the authority to make a diagnosis, with certain restrictions. The act points out that diagnosing, for a nurse, "means that identification of and discrimination between physical and psychosocial signs and symptoms essential to effective execution and management of the nursing regimen" [2]. The act does not authorize a nurse to make a medical diagnosis or prescribe medical therapeutic or corrective measures, except as may be authorized by the rules and regulations jointly promulgated by Pennsylvania's State Board of Medical Education and Licensure and State Board of Nurse Examiners [2].

Few cases have yet been decided by appellate courts of the United States involving the liabilities of a nurse in an expanded role under the new nurse practice acts or as a nurse-practitioner. Certain analogies may, however, be drawn from previous decisions involving nurses in their more traditional roles. If the same reasoning is used by the Courts in the future, the nurse acting as a nurse-practitioner or in an expanded role under the new legislation will still be measured against her peers in the determination of her personal liability, provided her actions have legal sanction. Experience has shown, however, that the future course of the law is unpredictable.

Violations of the Nurse Practice Act
Acting outside of the role provided for her in the nurse practice act may have serious consequences for a nurse.

1. A licensed nurse, acting in accord with her authority under the prevailing nurse practice act, who makes an incorrect nursing diagnosis as a result of which a patient is injured, may be sued and will be personally liable if it can be shown that she did not use the degree of skill and care prevalent among nurses of similar background in her community or a similar locale.

2. In the event that a nurse performs activities usually reserved for licensed *physicians* and not authorized for nurses under the prevailing nurse practice act, she will be personally liable if her patient is injured as a result of her failure to use that degree of care and skill prevalent among the *physicians* in her community [3, 4].

3. If a nurse's superior, whether it be a physician or a nurse supervisor, delegates a duty to a nurse that the superior would have been authorized to perform, and if the nurse is under the supervision or control of the superior in the performance of that duty, then the nurse's superior may be personally liable. Such liability could be based on negligent supervision by the supervisor of the nurse actually giving the care. Some cases have held hospitals responsible for providing nursing care or medical care of the standard provided by licensed professionals even when they have chosen to allow students to use their facility for clinical experience [5].

It should be pointed out that at least one widely cited opinion is an exception to what we believe to be the prevailing view in this developing field of law. *Thompson v. Brent* was decided by the Court of Appeal of Louisiana in 1971 on the following factual situation: In accord with the commonly accepted practice in his vicinity, a physician delegated the task of removing a cast with a Stryker saw to a medical assistant. The assistant continued to use the saw with an excessive amount of pressure, although the patient complained of pain and started to bleed. As a result, the patient's arm was cut and she sustained a residual scar approximately 4 inches long. The court held, in affirming a judgment for the plaintiff, that the assistant was required to use the same degree of care and skill as that prevalent among the physician's peers in the same community. We submit that this case would not apply today in most jurisdictions if an attempt were made to impose liability on a nurse rather than on her superior. It is more likely that a nurse, if she acted with legal sanction, that is, she acted within the scope of her Nurse Practice Act, would only be required to adhere to the standard of care and skill prevalent among her peers in the same community or in a similar locale. *Norton v. Argonaut Insurance Company,* an earlier case decided by the Louisiana Court of Appeal, seems to set forth the more reasonable rule, and one that we believe to be more generally applicable. In that case, the physician gave ambiguous written orders for the administration of Lanoxin to a 3-month-old infant. In the absence of specific directions from the physician, the nurse-defendant administered the drug to the infant by means of an injection rather than orally, with fatal results. The court stated in its opinion: "The duty of communication between physician and nurse is more important when we consider that the nurse who administers the medication is not held to the same degree of knowledge with respect thereto as the prescribing physician. . . ." [6, 7].

RESPONDEAT SUPERIOR

Roughly translated, *respondeat superior* means "let the master respond in damages." Of course the damages for which he must respond are those caused by the torts of his "servant" committed in the course of employment. As lawyers use the words *master* and *servant*, they have special meanings. In law, the word *master* refers to one who controls the physical conduct of another, his *servant*, in performing service for him. Conversely, the *servant* is a person employed to perform service for another in his affairs, and who, with respect to his physical conduct in performance of the service, is subject to the other's control or right to control.

In the relationship of master and servant, the employment does not require compensation, formal hiring, or a contract. Control does not mean complete control, and the servant is only required to respect the wishes of his superior, the master, regarding the manner of doing his job. A master is liable for the torts of his servant committed in the course of his employment. A tort is committed "in the course of his employment" when it is committed by a servant with the intention of furthering his master's ends rather than his own, and in a manner that does not vary too greatly from conduct which the master might foresee [8].

Respondeat superior is a legal theory that can be the basis of imposing liability on hospitals for injuries caused by the willful or negligent torts of their employees under certain circumstances.

It is not the theory under which a nurse supervisor is held liable for the torts of her subordinates. A nurse supervisor can be a staff nurse, team leader, head nurse, or administrator who controls the physical conduct of others in the performance of nursing duties for which she is primarily responsible. In order for the doctrine of respondeat superior to apply, a servant must be engaged in the master's business and attempting to further the master's ends. In general, a nurse supervisor is merely another employee or servant of the hospital, which is the master of both the supervisor and her subordinates. The supervisor is not an employer. The employer-hospital exercises control of the supervisor's subordinates through the supervisor, hence, such subordinates are not working for the supervisor on her affairs and are not her servants, even though she controls them [9].

A supervisor is liable for her own negligence in carrying out her supervisory duties, if such negligence results in injury to a patient. She may also impose liability on her employer for such negligence on the theory of respondeat superior.

Hence the health agency, or employer, may be held liable for the negligence of any of its employees. Although there is some authority for the proposition that nurses and physicians employed by a hospital are professionals and hence act as independent contractors, the present trend is to treat such individuals as servants, with their negligence imposing liability on the hospital-employer, which has an obligation to provide the patient with proper professional care [9]. The trend is also away from giving protection from suits for negligence to non-profit hospitals, under the doctrine of charitable immunity.

What are some circumstances in which a nurse supervisor could be held liable for injury to a patient? Certainly assigning the care of a patient to a staff nurse the supervisor knew to be inebriated would constitute negligence. If the patient was injured as a result, the supervisor would be liable for her own failure to use due care. The same reasoning would apply if a patient was injured because a nurse in a supervisory capacity assigned a staff nurse, LPN, or aide who was unqualified or incompetent for that particular patient assignment.

In regard to the kinds of acts or omissions by nurses that may result in imposition of liability on a hospital by virtue of respondeat superior, several observations may be made. Not only negligent torts, but also torts of a willful nature, such as false imprisonment and assault and battery, if committed in the course of a nurse's employment, may impose liability on her employer under the doctrine of respondeat superior.

It should also be added as a general proposition that commission of crimes by a servant is not a basis for imposing liability on the master. However, as we have pointed out, some crimes are also torts. In such a case, the same act could result in criminal and civil liability, and under certain circumstances, could also result in such civil liability being imposed on the employer of the person committing the act [8].

An example would be a nurse who gave unauthorized narcotics to a patient to relieve pain. If the patient was injured as a result, the nurse would be criminally liable for violating the controlled substances act. It could also be argued that the nurse's tortious act was committed in the course of her employment, thereby imposing civil liability on the hospital under the doctrine of respondeat superior.

Most of the cases involving imputed negligence do not concern the direct imposition of liability on nurses. Rather, they involve situations in which a nurse was negligent and an attempt was made by the plaintiff to recover damages from the hospital or physician for whom she worked. Perhaps the reason for this is that plaintiffs traditionally have felt that the hospital and physician had "fatter purses" and were more likely to be covered by liability insurance. In any event, this trend is changing with the rising status of the nursing profession. Nurses now constitute a more affluent class in our society. They not only have assets but are frequently covered by liability insurance. In the past, a patient who was forced to undergo an operation to retrieve a sponge left in him during previous surgery frequently sued the hospital, the surgeon, or both. The current trend seems to indicate that in such a situation the operating room nurse must also be prepared to be added to the list of defendants.

It seems proper to mention here the matter of malpractice insurance, which is dealt with in more detail in another chapter. It is possible that in the past plaintiffs felt that juries considered nurses economic "underdogs" and that involving them as defendants in a malpractice case would create antagonism for the plaintiff. This is no longer the case, and the nurse's exposure to lawsuits that attempt to impose liability directly on her has therefore greatly increased. The only real safeguard a nurse has against losses from this type of suit is adequate malpractice insurance.

WHITHER THE GOOD SAMARITAN?
It is almost axiomatic among physicians and other health professionals

such as nurses that stopping at the scene of an accident to render emergency care is an invitation to a lawsuit. Many authorities think that this basic assumption is completely false. Surely the chances for remuneration for this type of emergency service are limited, but the available statistics show that few lawsuits have been brought against nurses or physicians rendering this type of emergency care in good faith. If such lawsuits were in fact brought, the burden of pursuading a jury to award damages to such an ungrateful plaintiff would indeed be great [10]. In any event, the legislatures of the various states have recognized the need to encourage physicians, nurses, and others trained in the health care field to render emergency aid to victims of automobile accidents and other catastrophies. They have enacted what are commonly known as "good samaritan statutes." These statutes limit the liability of licensed practitioners of the healing arts in rendering emergency care at the scene of an accident to gross negligence or intentionally harmful acts, provided such care was rendered in good faith and in the belief that the situation did, in fact, constitute an emergency. From a strictly legal point of view, these acts offer little additional protection to the person rendering the emergency care. All a lawyer need do is plead gross negligence rather than simple negligence and the claim may still be one which must be resolved by a jury trial [10]. We believe that a nurse may better protect herself against whatever risks are actually involved in rendering emergency care at the scene of an accident by obtaining adequate professional liability, or malpractice, insurance [10].

REFERENCES

1. Hersey, Nathan. Prudence and the coffee break. *Am. J. Nurs.* 70:2389, 1970.
2. House Bill No. 129, Session of 1973, Act 151 of 1974, Commonwealth of Pennsylvania.
3. Barber v. Reiking. 411 P.2d 861 (Wash., 1966).
4. Hersey, Nathan. Standards of performance in expanded practice. *Am. J. Nurs.* 72:88, Jan. 1972.
5. Christensen v. Des Moines Still College of Osteopathy and Surgery et al. Supreme Court of Iowa, May 7, 1957.
6. Thompson v. Brent, Court of Appeal of Louisiana, Fourth Circuit. March 8, 1971.
7. Norton et al. v. Argonaut Insurance Company et al. No. 5601, Court of Appeal of Louisiana, First Circuit, June 29, 1962.
8. Mechem, Floyd R. *Outlines of the law of agency* (4th Ed). Chicago: Callaghan & Company, 1952. Chap. XII.
9. Mechem, Chapter XIV.
10. Busacca, Joseph F. Pennsylvania's Good Samaritan Statute—An answer to the medical profession's dilemma. *Villanova Law Rev.* 10:130, 1964.

6. CRIMES

Nurses, like all other citizens, are subject to the laws pertaining to crimes and have the same interests as other law-abiding citizens in the orderly and effective administration of criminal justice. *Miller on Criminal Law*, a well-known law school text, contains the following definition of a crime:

A crime may be generally defined as the commission or omission of an act which the law forbids or commands under pain of a punishment to be imposed by the state by a proceeding in its own name. In most cases the law requires that the commission or omission of the act must be accompanied by an unlawful intent [1].

CRIMINAL INTENT IN CRIMES AND TORTS

A crime is therefore an act denounced or proscribed by the state. An act is not a crime unless the state declares it to be a crime. Generally, crimes require a particular state of mind which must coincide with the forbidden act. This particular state of mind is frequently referred to by lawyers as criminal intent and by law school professors as *mens rea*. The criminal intent must coincide with the forbidden act. Either one without the other does not constitute a crime. Certainly criminal intent alone would not constitute a crime without some overt action, since a person cannot be punished for his thoughts, however depraved, in a democratic society. A forbidden act or omission proscribed by the state as a crime will not be punished as such unless the person who committed the crime had the necessary criminal intent at the time the act was committed. What is this state of mind or criminal intent? The answer is that it varies from crime to crime. In certain instances, the criminal intent must be very specific and, in fact, is known by lawyers as specific intent.

An example would be the case of burglary. Burglary *is* considered a felony in common law. It consists of breaking and entering the dwelling place of another with the intent of committing a felony. If the person breaking and entering really intended to deliver a gift or commit some crime less than a felony, he would not be guilty of burglary. A specific intent to commit a felony is required for one to be guilty of that particular crime. Certain other crimes merely require that the forbidden act be willful, or intentional. An example of this would be perjury, in which a person intentionally makes a false statement under oath. The necessity to prove criminal intent is one of the distinctions that sets crimes apart from torts.

Generally, torts do not require willfulness or a specific intent. One can be guilty of a tort through sheer negligence and, in fact, negligence is one of the most frequent grounds on which actions for tort are brought in our courts. As we have discussed in a previous chapter, torts are private offenses for which the victim may be compensated by money damages. Crimes are acts denounced by the state that are such a threat to society that they are punished by fines, imprisonment, or death, without any regard to compensating the victim. A particular act or omission can be both a tort and a crime. In tort cases, the outcome of the criminal proceedings does not affect that of the civil proceedings, and vice versa.

SOURCES OF CRIMINAL LAW

Various sources form the basis by which society, through its legislatures or sovereigns, declares certain acts to be criminal and makes the actor subject to punishment. Certainly, the primary source of criminal law is reason. It does not take a student of philosophy to deduce that human beings cannot live together if they are allowed to kill, rape, and rob each other at will. Hence, such atrocious offenses against members of society are universally denounced as crimes. The conventions and customs indigenous to particular groups or geographic areas are also an important source of criminal law. The possession of marijuana, for instance, may be a crime in one country and not in another. Procuring or causing an abortion may be denounced as a crime in one country and be supported as part of a national population control program by another.

In the United States, the criminal laws are contained in criminal codes enacted by the state legislatures and by Congress, as well as in the local ordinances of the various municipalities. However, the basis for these laws is generally the unwritten common law of Great Britain. By *unwritten* we do not mean that the opinions of the various common-law judges were not in writing. Of course they were. However, students of the law, in making a fine point, have stated that these opinions do not actually constitute the common law, but are rather evidence of what it is. There are no federal common-law crimes. Crimes not denounced by a federal statute are not punished in the federal district courts. In theory, the individual states may punish citizens for common-law crimes not contained in the statutes; however, this rarely, if ever, occurs. Theoretically, a violation of the state constitution may also constitute a crime. Nevertheless, the vast majority of crimes denounced and punished by the individual states are set forth in statutory form in the state criminal code [2].

EX POST FACTO CRIMES

Section 9 of article I of the Federal Constitution enumerates the powers denied to Congress. In clause 3 of section 9 it is stated that "No bill of attainder or ex post facto law shall be passed." An *ex post facto* law is a law denouncing and punishing as a crime an act that has already been committed. In other words, it is a retrospective law affecting acts or transactions that were not crimes at the time they occurred. The fact that retrospective criminal laws were far from unknown in Europe and Great Britain impelled the authors of the Constitution to include a prohibition against ex post facto laws. For the same reason, this prohibition has been incorporated in the constitutions of the various individual states [3].

CATEGORIES OF CRIMES

Certain acts are so evil and so atrocious, and in fact so contrary to the principles of an ordered society, that they are universally denounced as crimes. This category includes such crimes as murder, arson, robbery, maiming, and rape. Such crimes that involve acts which may be said to be inherently evil are called crimes *mala in se.*

Another category comprises acts or omissions that are not inherently evil, do not shock the conscience, and are only crimes because for reasons of its own a legislature has denounced them as such. Examples of such crimes would be failure to file an income tax return, violation of the antitrust laws, violation of labeling laws, or violation of any of a myriad of statutes provided for the orderly functioning and administration of an extremely complex society. Such crimes are called crimes *mala prohibita.* Sometimes the distinction between the two types of crime is difficult to draw, but it is nonetheless important. The distinction between crimes mala in se and crimes mala prohibita becomes particularly important in the matter of *constructive intent.*

Constructive Intent

A third type of intent will sometimes satisfy the need for the requisite mental element to make a prohibita act or omission a crime. This is known as constructive intent. In a sense, it is a fiction created by legislators and judges for reasons of public policy. Constructive intent is the intent attributed to a person who accidentally or inadvertently commits a crime malum in se while attempting and intending to commit another such crime. For example, a man who attempts to shoot his wife and accidentally shoots and kills his mother-in-law would be guilty of murdering his mother-in-law. The intent necessary to make the killing of the mother-in-law a murder is derived constructively from the intent that existed in the attempt to kill the wife.

There are certain requirements and limitations surrounding the finding of constructive intent by the courts:

1. The intended act must have been a crime malum in se rather than a crime malum prohibitum. For instance, there are cases that hold that an accidental killing in the course of exceeding the statutory speed limit is not murder, and that the constructive intent necessary to make such a killing a

murder should not be imputed from the intended crime, namely speeding, since such an act is not inherently evil and is a crime malum prohibitum rather than a crime malum in se [4].

2. Another limitation on the courts in finding constructive intent is that constructive intent cannot exist for crimes requiring specific intent. For instance, a defendant charged with assault with intent to commit murder was acquitted when the evidence indicated that he might actually have intended to kill a dog [5, 6, 7].

INCREASED MOBILITY AND UNIFORM LAWS

In the early history of the United States, the average American seldom traveled far from his home. If he made a journey to another state, it was frequently to move his household permanently and was a "once in a lifetime" adventure. In the nineteenth and twentieth centuries, with the technological explosion, the mobility of our population has skyrocketed. Americans frequently travel long distances in the course of their business or on vacations, and crossing state lines for Americans today is as common an experience as crossing county lines was for their forefathers a century ago.

This increasing mobility of the American population has made inconsistencies in the criminal laws of the various states an increasing problem. Drinking alcoholic beverages is legal in one state and not in another. Before the imposition of a national speed limit, 70 miles per hour might have been legal in one state and illegal in another. Most of the glaring inconsistencies have involved crimes that are mala prohibita. But even in the case of atrocious felonies that are crimes mala in se, such as murder, robbery, and rape, penalties vary widely from state to state.

THE MODEL PENAL CODE

A group of lawyers, judges, and legal scholars dedicated to creating more uniform laws throughout the United States is known as the American Law Institute. Through its efforts a number of model acts have been promulgated, among them the *Model Penal Code*. This code attempts to incorporate the best features of the criminal laws of the various states. A number of states have drawn on the *Model Penal Code* in varying degrees.

One of the most important provisions of the new code is the redefinition of crimes. Without attempting to change the substance of the criminal law generally prevailing in the United States, the code has attempted to redefine crimes in clear and unambiguous language that can be readily understood by both laymen and lawyers. It contains the following general statement of purposes:

(1) The general purposes of the provisions governing the definition of
offenses are:
  (a) To forbid and prevent conduct that unjustifiably and inexcusably
      inflicts or threatens substantial harm to individual or public
      interests;
  (b) To subject to public control persons whose conduct indicates that
      they are disposed to commit crimes;
  (c) To safeguard conduct that is without fault from condemnation as
      criminal;
  (d) To give fair warning of the nature of the conduct declared to con-
      stitute an offense;
  (e) To differentiate on reasonable grounds between serious and minor
      offenses***[8].

Few can argue with these commendable goals which seem to echo the
intent of the authors of the fifth amendment to the Federal Constitution,
which provides that "No person shall be. . . deprived of life, liberty, or
property, without due process of law. . . ." We believe that the *Model
Penal Code* will be an important influence on the development of criminal
law in the United States. For this reason, it would be valuable to take a
closer look at the definitions of crimes and offenses contained in this code.

Larceny
Larceny, commonly referred to by the public as stealing, is one of the most
common crimes to come before our courts. It was a felony in English
common law and was often punished by hanging in England and other
parts of the world prior to the nineteenth century. In common law, larceny
was defined as the unlawful taking and carrying away of the property of
another with the intent to permanently deprive him of his interest therein.
In legal terminology the intent necessary for the crime, which is a specific
intent to permanently deprive another of his interest in the stolen property,
is known as *animus furandi*. The necessary taking and carrying away is
referred to as *caption* and *asportation*. The property or subject matter of a
theft must be personal property, as opposed to real estate. It must be
personal property at the time it is stolen, and there have been cases which
have held that a person taking ore from another's mine was not guilty of
committing a larceny, since the ore was real estate at the time of the taking
and carrying away, which were both part of one continuous transaction [9,
10]. The element of taking and carrying away may exist even though there
is a very slight physical movement of the subject matter of the theft. For
instance, a thief who grasps a plate in a store and lifts it one-half inch off
the counter with the intent of unlawfully and permanently depriving the
store of its interest in the plate is guilty of larceny of the plate even though
he did not take it a great distance from its original location.

There are numerous varieties of simple larceny, but for the purposes of this book we will mention only a few. In English common law, cheating was obtaining the property of others with the intent to unlawfully and permanently deprive them of their interest in it by the use of false symbols or tokens. Obtaining money or goods by false pretenses or representations made with the intent to defraud is a statutory crime. If a false representation was involved it must be a false representation of either past or present facts. A mere representation of what will happen in the future such as a promise to pay in the future or a statement of opinion is not sufficient to provide the element necessary to the offense. For instance, a request for a loan of money, with the promise that the borrower is going to pay it back, is a representation about the future and, even though the loan is never repaid, the offense of committing larceny by false pretenses has not been committed. A mere promise to do something in the future is not a false pretense. Statements of opinion, even though false and exaggerated, are not sufficient to form an element of the crime of larceny by false pretense. For instance, a seller who exaggerates and puffs up the virtue of his goods for the purpose of selling them is not guilty of the offense. But, on the other hand, a jeweler attempting to sell a watch who knowingly and with intent to defraud claims that it has a solid gold case, when in fact he knows the case to be gold filled, is guilty of the crime of larceny by false pretense if he obtains money from the buyer for that watch as a result of the false representation [11, 12, 13].

Embezzlement

Embezzlement is a crime created by statute. It occurs when a person in lawful possession of property belonging to another fraudulently appropriates the property to himself or someone other than the owner. It does not constitute common-law larceny, because there is no taking and carrying away from the owner's possession. It is not necessary that the property had ever in fact been in the owner's possession. For example, an employee, such as a salesman, who received money from a customer and fraudulently appropriated it before it had ever reached his employer, would be guilty of embezzlement, as would an employee who received money from his employer to give to another and who fraudulently appropriated it to his own use.

Robbery

In English common law, robbery was a felony and consisted of taking and carrying away the personal property of another from his person or his presence with the intent to permanently and unlawfully deprive him of his interest therein, when such taking and carrying away was accomplished by violence or the threat of violence and against the will of the owner of the property. Thus it may be seen that robbery is larceny of personal property from the owner, or in his presence, using force or the threat of force. The force used may be very slight, as long as it overcomes the will of the property owner. A threat of force need not be of a nature that would intimidate a brave man, or even an average man or an average woman, but need only be sufficient to intimidate the owner of the property that was stolen.

In Miller's text, the crime of robbery is defined as ". . .a taking, against the will of the person from whom the property is taken" [14]. If the victim of a larceny is unconscious because of a blow from the thief at the time the property is taken, the thief is guilty of robbery, along with other crimes, since the absence of will on the part of the victim is due to the act of the thief or robber [14, 15]. In the case of the victim who is unconscious from voluntary intoxication, larceny from his person does not constitute robbery since the absence of will is caused by the victim himself.

Receiving Stolen Goods
One who takes into his possession stolen property, knowing that such property was stolen and with intent to deprive the owner of his interest therein, is guilty of a misdemeanor known in common law as receiving stolen goods, a crime closely related to larceny. In most states receiving stolen goods is made a felony by statute.

Generally, a person is charged with *constructive knowledge* that goods are stolen if they are offered to him at a price far below their market value or by someone who is a professional criminal. The intent required for this crime exists when the person receiving the goods intends to dispose of them in a manner inconsistent with the rights of the true owner. The property involved must be personal property or movable property, rather than real estate [16, 17, 18].

Under the *Model Penal Code*, which, in accord with its stated purposes, attempts "to give fair warning of the nature and conduct declared to constitute an offense," these various offenses against property are defined in clear and easily understandable language. For example, section 223.2, dealing with theft by unlawful taking or disposition, covers both real and personal property in the following manner:

(1) *Movable Property.* A person is guilty of theft if he takes, or exercises unlawful control over, movable property of another with purpose to deprive him thereof.
(2) *Immovable Property.* A person is guilty of theft if he unlawfully transfers immovable property of another or any interest therein with purpose to benefit himself or another not entitled thereto.

The crimes of larceny by false pretense, cheating by false pretense, and common-law cheating, with all their variations, are summarized and incorporated in section 223.3 of the *Model Penal Code*, which deals with theft by deception. This section provides that

A person is guilty of theft if he obtains property of another by deception. A person deceives if he purposely:
  (a) creates or reinforces a false impression, including false impressions as to law, value, intention or other state of mind; but deception as to a person's intention to perform a promise shall not be inferred from the fact alone that he did not subsequently perform the promise; or
  (b) prevents another from acquiring information which would affect his judgment of a transaction; or
  (c) fails to correct a false impression which the deceiver previously created or reinforced, or which the deceiver knows to be influencing another to whom he stands in a fiduciary or confidential relationship; or
  (d) fails to disclose a known lien, adverse claim or other legal impediment to the enjoyment of property which he transfers or encumbers in consideration for the property obtained, whether such impediment is or is not valid, or is or is not a matter of official record.
The term *deceive* does not, however, include falsity as to matters having no pecuniary significance, or puffing by statements unlikely to deceive ordinary persons in the group addressed.

The offense of receiving stolen property is defined in section 223.6 of the *Model Penal Code* as follows:

(1) *Receiving*. A person is guilty of theft if he receives, retains, or disposes of movable property of another knowing that it has been stolen, or believing that it has probably been stolen, unless the property is received, retained, or disposed with purpose to restore it to the owner. "Receiving" means acquiring possession, control or title, or lending on the security of the property.
(2) *Presumption of Knowledge*. The requisite knowledge of belief is presumed in the case of a dealer who:
  (a) is found in possession or control of property stolen from two or more persons on separate occasions; or
  (b) has received stolen property in another transaction within the year preceding the transaction charged; or
  (c) being a dealer in property of the sort received, acquires it for a consideration which he knows is far below its reasonable value.
"Dealer" means a person in the business of buying or selling goods.

The definition of robbery contained in section 222.1 of the *Model Penal Code* is somewhat deficient in our opinion, inasmuch as it does not relate to violence or the threat of violence in overcoming the will of the victim. In the Code, robbery is defined as follows:

(1) *Robbery Defined.* A person is guilty of robbery if, in the course of committing a theft, he:
  (a) inflicts serious bodily injury upon another; or
  (b) threatens another with or purposely puts him in fear of immediate serious bodily injury; or
  (c) commits or threatens immediately to commit any felony of the first or second degree.
An act shall be deemed "in the course of committing a theft" if it occurs in an attempt to commit theft or in flight after the attempt or commission [19].

Homicide

Homicide may be defined as the killing of one human being by another. It may be justifiable, excusable, or felonious [20]. In order for the act or omission of one human being causing the death of another human being to be called homicide, death must ensue within one year and one day from the act or omission [21]. The act or omission must have been a contributing proximate cause of death, although it need not have been the sole cause. Therefore, a blow that causes the death of a person already dying from disease constitutes homicide, and if the requisite intent is present it is considered murder.

A homicide may be justifiable or excusable. An example of a justifiable homicide is a homicide consummated in carrying out a legal duty, as in the case of a soldier who kills an enemy in the line of duty. It also may be a killing done in the course of carrying out a lawful order of a court, as in the case of a prison official who commits a homicide in the course of carrying out a lawful death sentence. Therefore, a homicide is justifiable when one person kills another in strict performance of a legal duty. Homicide will also be justifiable when deadly force is reasonably necessary to prevent a felony, suppress a riot, or prevent the escape of one who has committed a felony [22]. Self-defense by one who is in reasonable fear of grievous bodily harm or death may also be a justification for homicide. In the case of self-defense, a person in his or her dwelling place or place of business has no duty to retreat before using deadly force. In the minority view, when outside of his or her dwelling place or place of business, a person is required to retreat if reasonably possible before using deadly force in self-defense [23].

Excusable homicide is homicide by accident. A person who causes the death of another must have been engaged in a lawful act and using due care at the time of the accident. Under certain circumstances deadly force, used in self-defense, that results in the death of another person may be excusable, but not justifiable. An example would be the case of a person who allows himself to be drawn into a fight that he might otherwise have avoided and then suddenly finds himself confronted with an attempt by his adversary to take his life or inflict grievous bodily harm. If, under those circumstances, it is reasonably necessary for him to use deadly force to save his own life or prevent grievous bodily harm to himself, even though he should not have involved himself in the fight in the first place, the resulting homicide will be excusable [24].

The distinction between justifiable and excusable homicide is difficult to make and purely academic at this stage in the development of the law, since no criminal penalties are imposed for either act. The distinction still exists in courses in criminal law; however, the current tendency is to combine both classical distinctions under the category of justifiable homicide, which is in fact done in the *Model Penal Code* in article III, sections 3.01-3.04:

Section 3.03. Execution of Public Duty.

(1) Except as provided in Subsection (2) of this Section, conduct is justifiable when it is required or authorized by:
   (a) the law defining the duties or functions of a public officer or the assistance to be rendered to such officer in the performance of his duties; or
   (b) the law governing the execution of legal process; or
   (c) the judgment or order of a competent court or tribunal; or
   (d) the law governing the armed services or the lawful conduct of war; or
   (e) any other provision of law imposing public duty.
(2) The other sections of this Article apply to:
   (a) the use of force upon or toward the person of another for any of the purposes dealt with in such sections; and
   (b) the use of deadly force for any purpose, unless the use of such force is otherwise expressly authorized by law or occurs in the lawful conduct of war.
(3) The justification afforded by Subsection (1) of this Section applies:
   (a) when the actor believes his conduct to be required or authorized by the judgment or direction of a competent court or tribunal or in lawful execution of legal process, notwithstanding lack of jurisdiction of the court or defect in the legal process; and
   (b) when the actor believes his conduct to be required or authorized to assist a public officer in his performance of his duties, notwithstanding that the officer exceeded his legal authority.

Section 3.04. Use of Force in Self-Protection.

(2) *Limitations on Justifying Necessity for Use of Force.*
   (b) The use of deadly force is not justifiable under this Section unless the actor believes that such force is necessary to protect himself against death, serious bodily harm, kidnapping or sexual intercourse compelled by force or threat; nor is it justifiable if:
      (i) the actor, with the purpose of causing death or serious bodily harm, provoked the use of force against himself in the same encounter; or

   (ii) the actor knows that he can avoid the necessity of using such force with complete safety by retreating or by surrendering possession of a thing to a person asserting a claim of right thereto or by complying with a demand that he abstain from any action which he has no duty to take, except that:
      (1) the actor is not obliged to retreat from his dwelling or place of work, unless he was the initial aggressor or is assailed in his place of work by another person whose place of work the actor knows it to be; and
      (2) a public officer justified in using force in the performance of his duties or a person justified in using force in his assistance or a person justified in using force in making an arrest or preventing an escape is not obliged to desist from efforts to perform such duty, effect such arrest or prevent such escape because of resistance or threatened resistance by or on behalf of the person against whom such action is directed.
   (c) Except as required by paragraphs (a) and (b) of this Subsection, a person employing protective force may estimate the necessity thereof under the circumstances as he believes them to be when the force is used, without retreating, surrendering possession, doing any other act which he has no legal duty to do or abstaining from any lawful action.

Murder

Any homicide committed without justification or excuse is criminal homicide and a felony. Criminal homicide may be divided into two general categories: murder and manslaughter. Killing another person with malice aforethought is murder. The words *malice aforethought* imply an evil intent and premeditation. In fact, premeditation is only theoretical. The evil intent is supplied under the following circumstances:

1. Whenever the person doing the killing intends to kill or inflict grievous bodily harm on another person, whether it is the one actually killed or not. For example, a man attempting to shoot his wife who inadvertently kills his child is guilty of murder [25].

2. A killing in the course of committing a felony, whether or not death or grievous bodily harm to anyone was intended, constitutes murder. For instance, a burglar who, in the course of burglarizing a house, awakens an occupant who in turn inadvertently shoots and kills another occupant, is guilty of murder.

3. One who commits an act so reckless and dangerous that it will probably cause the death or serious bodily injury of another is guilty of murder if another is killed thereby. Therefore, in the case of a man who threw a heavy beer glass toward his wife and broke a lighted lamp carried by her, scattering burning oil over her clothes and causing her death, the Supreme Court of Illinois found the evidence sufficient to constitute an act of murder [26, 27, 28].

When a police officer or other person with similar authority acts in his official capacity, he is placed in a special status by the law. If he is killed by one resisting him while he is engaged in making a lawful arrest, the resisting person is guilty of murder. This is so even though, because of provocation or lack of premeditation, the crime would have been reduced to manslaughter if the victim had not been a police officer acting in execution of his duty. The same criteria apply if the person killed is either a private citizen or police officer attempting to suppress a riot and the killer was one resisting such efforts [29].

What we have been talking about up to this point is the element of malice in malice aforethought. As to the element of premeditation, no particular amount of time for reflection is necessary. Premeditation may occur in a moment. It is sufficient to satisfy this requirement that the act or omission causing death be deliberate, whether or not the ensuing result is. For example, a person who, on impulse, deliberately threw a heavy typewriter out of a fourth-story window over a crowded street would be guilty of the murder of a pedestrian killed thereby, whether he intended to hurt anyone or not.

In various jurisdictions throughout the United States, murder is divided into several degrees. Where this is done, first-degree murder is usually defined as murder involving an attempt to kill or do grievous bodily harm to someone, which results in the death of the intended victim or another. First-degree murder usually includes all homicides committed in the course of perpetrating an atrocious felony such as murder, robbery, rape, or arson. Second-degree murder would include murder that does not rise to the level of first-degree murder, such as homicide resulting from a wantonly reckless and dangerous act or homicide committed in the course of perpetrating a felony other than an atrocious felony.

With slightly different wording, the *Model Penal Code* preserves the substance of the criminal law pertaining to murder prevailing throughout the United States. In section 210.1 of the *Model Penal Code* the following definition of criminal homicide is given.

(1) A person is guilty of criminal homicide if he purposely, knowingly, recklessly or negligently causes the death of another human being.
(2) Criminal homicide is murder, manslaughter or negligent homicide.

The crime of murder undivided by degrees is defined in section 210.2 of the *Model Penal Code* as follows:

(1) Except as provided in Section 210.3(1) (b), criminal homicide constitutes murder when:
    (a) it is committed purposely or knowingly; or
    (b) it is committed recklessly under circumstances manifesting extreme indifference to the value of human life. Such recklessness

and indifference are presumed if the actor is engaged or is an accomplice in the commission of, or an attempt to commit, or flight after committing or attempting to commit robbery, rape or deviate sexual intercourse by force or threat of force, arson, burglary, kidnapping or felonious escape.

(2) Murder is a felony of the first degree [but a person convicted of murder may be sentenced to death, as provided in Section 210.6].

The exception referred to in section 210.2(1) is made in the case of a mental element that would reduce murder to voluntary manslaughter.

Manslaughter

Manslaughter is generally classified as either voluntary or involuntary. Voluntary manslaughter is the intentional killing of another that would constitute the crime of murder were it not for the fact that malice is lacking. This is another way of saying that the fatal act was committed in the heat of passion and on adequate provocation. When the courts use the term *adequate provocation*, they are not referring to the type of factual circumstance that would justify or excuse a killing; rather they mean a situation that would infuriate or enrage the average citizen to the point at which he would lose his reason and self-control. Provocation must cause the passion or fury, and the passion or fury must cause the fatal act in order to reduce to voluntary manslaughter the killing that would otherwise be considered murder. No appreciable time interval may exist between the provocation and the act. If there is a sufficient time interval between the provocation and the act, during which a reasonable man might regain his self-control, the test for reducing murder to voluntary manslaughter has not been met [30].

Adequate provocation has been held to include finding one's spouse in an act of adultery, a father seeing his daughter whipped by his son-in-law [31], and great insults and abusive language. For example, a wife who came home from the hospital and found her husband in bed with the woman who lived next door might, if she was enraged at the sight and immediately shot them both, be convicted of voluntary manslaughter rather than murder. However, if she went home to her mother and father and discussed the whole thing, whipping herself into a fury over the injustice of her husband's actions, and then went back and shot him, she would be guilty of murder. A broader and more enlightened definition of the mental state necessary to reduce murder to voluntary manslaughter is given in the *Model Penal Code* in which manslaughter is defined as follows:

A homicide which would otherwise be murder is committed under the influence of extreme mental or emotional disturbance for which there is reasonable explanation or excuse. The reasonableness of such explanation or excuse shall be determined from the viewpoint of a person in the actor's situation under the circumstances as he believes them to be [32].

Involuntary manslaughter is, in a sense, analogous to second-degree murder, since it is unintentional killing by culpable negligence or recklessness. But it lacks a sufficient degree of wantonness to consitute second-degree murder. Involuntary manslaughter is also a killing in the course of an unlawful act that is malum in se but does not constitute a felony. For instance, an individual who causes the death of another while driving his automobile recklessly may be found guilty of involuntary manslaughter. Reckless driving is generally a misdemeanor rather than a felony and it is a crime malum in se. If the recklessness was of an extreme variety such as driving through a crowd of people at a high rate of speed, the driver might be guilty of second-degree murder. Conversely, it could be argued that a person who is involved in an accident in which he kills another while hunting without a license would not be guilty of involuntary manslaughter if his conduct was not culpably negligent or reckless. In view of the foregoing, it is interesting to speculate on whether a nurse whose patient died as a result of treatment she gave in good faith, outside of the parameters of the nursing practice act of her state, would be guilty of involuntary manslaughter if she did not act recklessly, negligently, or with lack of skill.

THE NURSE AS POTENTIAL MURDERER
Euthanasia and abortion are two areas in which the professional nurse may be confronted with the possibility of committing the crime of murder.

Euthanasia
Euthanasia may be either passive or active, voluntary or involuntary. Passive euthanasia is, in effect, euthanasia by default or omission. It occurs when one responsible for the care of another deliberately omits rendering such care with the humanitarian purpose of shortening the life of one who is terminally ill and suffering from intractable pain. In a case in which the care omitted is of such a nature that the nurse or other health care professional had a legal duty to provide it under the circumstances, deliberate omission of such care with the intention of shortening life or causing death is considered murder if death ensues within one year and one day from the omission.

In the case of active euthanasia, the nurse or other health care professional would be guilty of murder if, instead of an omission, she or he performed an affirmative act, such as giving excessive dosages of a narcotic, with the intention of shortening or terminating the life of a terminally ill patient, if as a result the patient's death ensued within one year and one day of the affirmative act.

Voluntary euthanasia is euthanasia, whether passive or active, performed at the request of the patient while the patient still has command of his or her mental faculties. Involuntary euthanasia is euthanasia performed on an incompetent or comatose patient. In either case the request by the patient or the mental state of the patient is no defense to the person performing the euthanasia, and the crime is still murder in all jurisdictions in the United States. This is not to say that many health care professionals have been prosecuted for murder under such circumstances if their motive was humanitarian and the patient was suffering and terminally ill. But, in spite of the fact that the cases involving such prosecutions are almost nonexistent, the fact remains that anyone, whether a nurse or a physician, who becomes involved in euthanasia exposes himself or herself to the risk of criminal prosecution. A nurse who performs an act or omission constituting euthanasia, even though under the orders of a physician, is guilty of murder if she knows that the act or omission will result in her patient's death.

Abortion

In the area of abortion, in the case of *Roe v. Wade* [33], the Supreme Court of the United States recently ruled that, during the first trimester of pregnancy, the decision to have an abortion is to be left to the medical judgment of the pregnant woman's physician and that the state may not intervene. After the first trimester of pregnancy, state laws may regulate abortion procedures in a way related to maternal health. The opinion in the Roe case further provided that after the fetus becomes "viable," or has a chance of surviving outside of the womb, the state may regulate or even forbid abortion "except where necessary, in appropriate medical judgement, for the preservation of the life or health of the mother" [33].

Previous to *Roe v. Wade*, a death caused while procuring or causing an abortion was proscribed as a felony. Today, it would still be possible for a nurse to be prosecuted for murder for aiding in an abortion that resulted in the death of the mother, if the abortion fell outside of the Supreme Court guidelines and occurred in a state which denounced procuring an abortion as a felony.

A more sensitive area, and one in which the law is still developing and unresolved, is the question of fetal death, or *when* a fetus becomes a human being capable of being murdered. As a result of the proliferation of abortions and abortion clinics, many fetuses are born alive and breathe, kick, squirm, and cry before they finally die. Is a doctor or nurse guilty of murder when he or she fails to treat the fetus and keep it alive, even though its chances for survival are practically nonexistent? Is a nurse or doctor guilty of murder when he or she handles or treats the fetus in such a way as to hasten its death? The cases seem to indicate that any fetus that has an independent circulation from its mother or that is in a viable stage of its development and in the process of being delivered from its mother's body is a human being capable of being murdered [34].

If the anti-abortion movement in the United States gains sufficient momentum and power, we believe that the courts will eventually hold that such fetuses are human beings, and that health care professionals who are responsible for their care will ultimately be treated as murderers if they deliberately fail to take reasonable measures in an attempt to help these "viable" fetuses survive.

RAPE

Rape is generally defined as a crime committed by a man and involves unlawful carnal knowledge of a woman by force and against her will. In order to understand the crime it is necessary to analyze each of its essential elements:

1. Only a man is capable of actually committing the crime of rape. However, under some circumstances, a woman may aid and abet a man in committing a rape. She then becomes an accessory *before the fact* and in some jurisdictions is subject to punishment for rape as if she were an actual rapist.

2. In order for carnal knowledge of a woman to constitute a rape, it is essential that it be unlawful. Therefore, a man cannot rape his own wife, since all intercourse with a spouse is lawful per se. It is possible for a man to aid and abet another in raping his wife, in which case he would be guilty either as an accessory before the fact or as a principal.

3. The carnal knowledge which forms an essential element of the crime of rape constitutes the slightest penetration of the victim's reproductive organs, whether or not emission takes place.

4. The force required as an element of rape may be actual or constructive. It is closely related to the other essential element, which is lack of consent. In the case of a woman in possession of her faculties who has reached "the age of consent," at which she is legally considered capable of consenting to sexual intercourse, the force required for rape is the force sufficient to overcome the woman's resistance. However, the victim's resistance is not required to be to the extreme limit of her physical capability, but need only be of a degree or character to show unwillingness up to the time of actual penetration. Force sufficient to overcome such resistance is force sufficient to constitute the crime of rape [35].

Under certain circumstances, actual force beyond the force inherent in any sexual intercourse is not required to complete the crime of rape. This would be the case if the victim were unconscious, less than 10 years old under common law, or under the age of consent set by statute in a particular jurisdiction. It would also be the case if the consent of the victim was obtained by threats and fear of death or bodily injury. The actual force beyond the force necessary to complete the act would not be required if the victim had a mental impairment that prevented her from knowing what she was doing, and the man having intercourse with her knew of her infirmity.

5. An essential element of rape is that the unlawful sexual intercourse be against the woman's will. Lack of consent is implied if the woman is asleep, unconscious, or if she submits from fear caused by threats of immediate bodily harm to herself or another.

Although cases involving consent obtained by fraud are rare in contemporary society, perhaps due to our increasing sophistication, there are a number of older cases declaring that a woman who consents to have intercourse with one impersonating her husband, who she actually believes to be her husband, has in fact been raped. The majority of cases hold that when consent to an act of intercourse is obtained by fraud, the crime is not rape, since the fraud was to a collateral matter and not to the nature of the act that actually took place. However, the general view is that a woman has been raped when she believes that she is submitting to a surgical operation by a physician who has sexual relations with her instead. The reasoning is that she consented to an entirely different act. Bizarre as this set of circumstances may seem, there are a number of cases involving such situations [36].

The *Model Penal Code*, in section 213.1 dealing with rape and related offenses, sets forth the definition of the crime that embodies the common-law and generally prevailing view in this country and, in addition, acknowledges the problems involved in our present drug culture by providing that the requisite lack of consent for rape exists if a man substantially impairs his victim's power to control her conduct through the use of drugs or intoxicants. In subparagraph 2(a) of section 213.1, the Code sets forth a broader definition of the type of threat which will be a substitute for actual force and vitiate the victim's consent. It is provided that "any threat that would prevent resistance by a woman of ordinary resolution" will suffice.

Section 213.1 Rape and Related Offenses.

(1) *Rape.* A male who has sexual intercourse with a female not his wife is guilty of rape if:
   (a) he compels her to submit by force or by threat of imminent death, serious bodily injury, extreme pain or kidnapping, to be inflicted on anyone; or
   (b) he has substantially impaired her power to appraise or control her conduct by administering or employing without her knowledge drugs, intoxicants or other means for the purpose of preventing resistance; or
   (c) the female is unconscious; or

(d) the female is less than 10 years old.

Rape is a felony of the second degree unless (i) in the course thereof the actor inflicts serious bodily injury upon anyone, or (ii) the victim was not a voluntary social companion of the actor upon the occasion of the crime and had not previously permitted him sexual liberties, in which cases the offense is a felony of the first degree. Sexual intercourse includes intercourse per os or per anum, with some penetration however slight; emission is not required.

(2) *Gross Sexual Imposition.* A male who has sexual intercourse with a female not his wife commits a felony of the third degree if:

   (a) he compels her to submit by any threat that would prevent resistance by a woman of ordinary resolution; or

   (b) he knows that she suffers from a mental disease or defect which renders her incapable of appraising the nature of her conduct; or

   (c) he knows that she is unaware that a sexual act is being committed upon her or that she submits because she falsely supposes that he is her husband.

DEVIATE SEXUAL INTERCOURSE

Sodomy encompasses carnal copulation by the mouth or the anus between man and man or man and woman, or any carnal copulation by a man or a woman with a beast. The word *sodomy* is derived from the biblical city of Sodom where such vices were prevalent and which, because of its sinfulness, was destroyed by fire. Bestiality refers only to carnal copulation between a man or a woman and a beast and is therefore encompassed by, but not synonymous with, sodomy.

"The abominable and detestable crime against nature" is a phrase frequently applied to the acts encompassed by the crime of sodomy. These acts are generally treated as felonies under English common law and have been in the past defined by statute as felonies [37]. The present trend is to make private deviate sexual relations between consenting adults noncriminal. In fact the Practicing Law Institute voted against including private homosexuality that does not involve force, imposition, or corruption of the young as an offense in the *Model Penal Code*. Section 213.2 of the Code deals only with deviate sexual intercourse by force or imposition.

FORNICATION AND ADULTERY

Both fornication and adultery are crimes dealing with voluntary but unlawful sexual intercourse. Adultery has different meanings in different jurisdictions. Originally, it was not a crime under common law but was punished in the ecclesiastical courts, being an offense against morals and religion rather than a crime. Although definitions of the offense vary, under all the definitions at least one party to the illicit sexual intercourse must be married. In some states, when a man and a woman have voluntary illicit sexual intercourse and one is married, both are guilty of adultery. In other states, only the party or parties to the illicit sexual union who are married are guilty of adultery. In still other states, it is essential that a married woman have intercourse with a man other than her spouse in order to have committed the crime of adultery, in which case both parties are guilty of the offense. A person is considered married and capable of committing the offense of adultery if his or her divorce decree has not become final.

Under Roman law it was necessary for the crime of adultery that the woman be married and have intercourse with a person other than her spouse. A married man having intercourse with an unmarried woman was not considered guilty of adultery. The rationale behind this was that the law against adultery was designed to protect husbands from the necessity of supporting other men's children. The prevailing view is that an unmarried woman who has intercourse with a married man does not commit adultery, while a married woman having intercourse with a man other than her husband is guilty of adultery.

Another variation in the statutes throughout the United States involves the necessity for more than a single act of sexual intercourse to constitute the crime. In states where the act making adultery a crime uses such language as "living in adultery or fornication," more than a single act of sexual intercourse is required. Generally speaking, states in which the statute does not use such language require only a single act to constitute the offense [38].

Fornication is unlawful sexual intercourse between consenting unmarried persons, and does not constitute adultery. While it was not a crime under common law, it has been made so by statute in many of the states. The current trend is to make both fornication and adultery noncriminal. In recognition of this trend, the *Model Penal Code* does not treat such acts as crimes. Even where such acts are proscribed as crimes, criminal sanctions are rarely, if ever, imposed against the offenders.

While we take no position regarding the moral and ethical considerations involved, it cannot be argued that retaining statutes that are almost universally ignored encourages respect for our courts or facilitates the administration of criminal justice.

NARCOTICS

A large proportion of the cases passing through our criminal courts today involve the use or possession of narcotics, or are drug-related. Since a nurse is frequently called on to dispense and handle narcotics, it is important that she be familiar with the laws pertaining to narcotics in her state. There is a wide disparity throughout the United States in the penalties imposed for illegal use, possession, or sale of narcotics, which are frequently referred to as controlled substances.

In some states the possession of the most common narcotic, marijuana, is a felony and in others it is a misdemeanor. In an attempt to bring some uniformity to this important field of law, numerous states have adopted the Uniform Controlled Dangerous Substances Act or the Uniform Narcotic Drug Act. In all states the dispensing, prescribing, and sale of addictive drugs are controlled by statute. In almost every state the possession of a narcotic not acquired within the scope of an applicable statute is a crime, and frequently a felony. Illegal selling is invariably punished more severely than possession. In Pennsylvania, the following law applies:

Any person who is at least 21 years of age and who is not himself a drug dependent person who violates this Act by distributing a controlled substance. . .to a person under 18 years of age who is at least four years his junior is punishable by a term of imprisonment up to twice that otherwise authorized . . .[39].

In most jurisdictions, repeat offenders are punished more severely than first offenders for any act related to the use, possession, or sale of drugs. While the possession of marijuana has not yet been generally decriminalized, in some states possession of a small amount of marijuana for personal use, or distribution (*not* sale) of a small amount of marijuana, is treated as a misdemeanor rather than a felony.

Practical Considerations for Nurses
in Handling Narcotics

Nurses are prohibited by law from dispensing narcotics, except under the direction and supervision of a licensed physician or dentist. Administering drugs is a duty nurses are frequently required to perform, especially in hospitals. Numerous safeguards and control measures are incorporated in the standard operating procedures of every well-run hospital. Traditionally, there is a narcotics count at the changing of each nursing shift. Hospital regulations usually provide that all narcotics refused by a patient or otherwise rendered unusable must be accounted for, and a written record made of their disposition. Hospitals may have rules setting the time limit on the validity of a p.r.n. (pro re nata, or according to need) order for a narcotic drug. Although under certain circumstances a verbal order prescribing a narcotic is legal, it certainly is in the interest of the nurse dispensing the drug to make a note of the order and the description of the circumstances under which it was ordered on the chart and to have the prescribing physician validate the order as soon as possible.

The Massachusetts General Hospital in its *Manual of Nursing Procedures* sets these fairly typical guidelines for dispensing narcotics:

(15) Narcotic Sheet:
   (a) Narcotic medications are to be dispensed from medicine closet only.
   (b) Narcotic orders are valid until 12 noon on the second day after they are written.
   (c) Narcotics are not to be given if respirations are below 12 per minute. Respirations should be counted before preparing a narcotic dose.
(16) Controlled Drugs:
   (a) Control drugs include all stimulant, depressant, and hallucinogenic drugs, e.g., amphetimines, barbiturates, tranquilizers, sedatives.
   (b) Control drugs are not to be located in an easily accessible or visible area on the medicine cart. These medications will be stored locked either on the cart or in the supplemental medicine closet or main closet [40].

In summary, the strict sanctions imposed on the improper use of narcotics make it mandatory that, in addition to complying with the laws applicable to controlled substances, nurses follow all hospital procedures pertaining to narcotics carefully. It is essential that they thoroughly chart all verbal orders from physicians that call for the dispensing of narcotics.

REFERENCES
1. Miller, Justin. *Handbook of criminal law.* St. Paul, Minn.: West Publishing Co., 1934. P. 16.
2. Miller, pp. 30-32.
3. LaFaure, Wayne R., and Scott, Austin W., Jr. *Handbook of criminal law.* St. Paul, Minn.: West Publishing Co., 1972. Pp. 89-93.
4. Jackson v. State. 101 Ohio St. 152, 127 N.E. 870 (1920). Cited in Miller, p. 63.
5. Miller, pp. 61-65.
6. LaFaure, p. 202.
7. People v. Keefer. 18 Cal. 636 (1861). Cited in Miller, p. 64.
8. The Model Penal Code, Proposed Official Draft, May 4, 1962, American Law Institute, Sec. 1.02(1). Copyright 1967 by The American Law Institute. Reprinted with the permission of The American Law Institute.
9. People v. Williams, 35 Cal. 671 (1868). Cited in Miller, p. 345.
10. LaFaure, pp. 633, 634.
11. Miller, pp. 382-87.
12. Model Penal Code, Sec. 223.3.
13. LaFaure, pp. 657, 675.
14. Miller, p. 395.
15. LaFaure, p. 697.
16. Miller, pp. 396-400.
17. Model Penal Code, Sec. 223.6.
18. LaFaure, pp. 685-688.

19. Model Penal Code, Sec. 222.1.
20. Miller, p. 251.
21. LaFaure, p. 534.
22. Miller, pp. 255-262.
23. LaFaure, pp. 395-396.
24. Miller, p. 261.
25. LaFaure, pp. 535-541.
26. Miller, p. 268.
27. Mayes v. People, 106 Ill. 306, 46 Am. Rep. 698. (1883).
28. LaFaure, pp. 541-545.
29. LaFaure, pp. 561, 562.
30. LaFaure, pp. 572-582.
31. Campbell v. Com. 88 Ky. 402, 11 S.W. 290 (1889). Cited in Miller, p. 281.
32. Model Penal Code, Sec. 210.3(1)(b).
33. Roe et al. v. Wade, District Attorney of Dallas County, 410 U.S. 113 (1973).
34. LaFaure, pp. 530-532.
35. Miller, p. 295.
36. Miller, p. 299.
37. See discussion in Miller, Chap. 16, Sec. 141.
38. See discussion of Adultery and Fornication in Miller, Chap. 16, Secs. 136 and 137.
39. Title 35 Pennsylvania Statutes Annotated, Secs. 780-114.
40. Department of Nursing, Massachusetts General Hospital. *Massachusetts General Hospital manual of nursing procedures.* Boston: Little, Brown, 1975. P. 135.

7. NURSE PRACTICE ACTS

Like the Colonel's Lady and Judy O'Grady, who were sisters under their skins [1], the nurse in her traditional role has shared a kinship with the medieval nuns offering succor to the ill, and with the women caring for the wounded in the van of the countless armies that plundered their way across Europe. However, nursing in the United States has undergone a dramatic evolution as a result of the women's rights movement and the national health care crisis. The nurse has transcended the role of handmaiden to the physician to assume the role of an independent professional collaborating with other members of the health care team.

Nursing had no legal definition until the early 1900s when the state governments first recognized the need for nurses to have formal training and passed state nursing laws. In the original nursing acts of North Carolina, New Jersey, and New York, which were passed in 1903, there was no definition of nursing practice. Nurses functioned at this time only under the direction of physicians, so it is understandable that these original state acts established only the requirements for nursing education and licensing, the funds for administering the law, and the boards of nurse examiners in North Carolina and New York. At present, all states license professional nurses and, except for eight states and the District of Columbia, the practice of nursing is regulated by state nurse practice acts [2].

The need for a definition of nursing prompted the American Nurses' Association (ANA) to propose a model definition in 1955:

The practice of professional nursing means the performance for compensation of any act in the observation, care and counsel of the ill, injured, or infirm, or in the maintenance of health or prevention of illness of others, or in the supervision and teaching of other personnel, or the administration of medications and treatments prescribed by a licensed physician or dentist; requiring substantial specialized judgment and skill and based on knowledge and application of the principles of biological, physical and social sciences. The foregoing shall not be deemed to include acts of diagnosis or prescription of therapeutic or corrective measures [3].

In 1970, the Council of the ANA suggested an additional section for states in which law is strictly constructed.

A professional nurse may also perform such additional acts, under emergency or other special conditions, which may include special training, as are recognized by the medical and nursing professions as proper to be

65

performed by a professional nurse under such conditions, even though such acts might otherwise be considered diagnosis and prescription [3].

In the *Rules and Regulations of the Catoosa Hospital* in Griffin, Georgia, dated 1863, the role of the nurse was stated succinctly: "Nurses must obey strictly all orders from the surgeon and wardmasters of their ward" [4]. Whatever reception this order received from the Confederate ladies at Catoosa Hospital, such a submissive role would be totally unacceptable to nurses today. At present, nearly every state in the union is wrestling with promulgating or implementing a new nurse practice act. This is the first attempt by the nursing profession to define its body of knowledge and its area of practice. Nurses, to be certain, have given, and will give, a lot of guidance to legislators as they are called on to define nursing; but the other health professionals, the lay public, and the courts will also help delineate the nurse's area of practice.

All nursing decisions are not of the life-or-death variety and all nursing does not involve a right or wrong approach. There are areas in which nursing not only can, but must, question policies that have been handed down over the years. Through a process of assessment, planning, implementation, and evaluation, nursing problems can be met in an organized, controlled manner, and areas requiring nursing research can be delineated. The process must test nursing interventions, and nurses will learn from mistakes as well as from successes. At present, when nurses themselves do not totally understand what their area of practice is, such understanding cannot be expected of the lay public. A recent study shows the public image of nurses to be that of a "female nurturer, medicator, physician's assistant, and maid" [5]. It is evident that a nurse is unable to practice in a vacuum, disassociated from the public she serves. It is therefore critically important that current legislative decisions redefine the role of professional nursing. The new role must be disseminated to the public through the appropriate media so that the health consumer will be able to understand and fully utilize the "new product."

Licensing acts are designed to protect the lay public from incompetent practitioners. The Department of Health, Education, and Welfare Report of 1971 titled *Extending the Scope of Nursing Practice* acknowledges nurses as the health personnel most able to provide economically for health care needs in this country. Health today is considered a right; it means physical, mental, and social well-being rather than merely the absence of disease. Medical care and health care do not have the same meaning, and this is important to keep in mind when reading nurse practice acts.

The themes most frequently focused on in the new nurse practice acts throughout the United States are: (1) definition of nursing, (2) composition and responsibilities of the state board of nursing, (3) licensure requirements, (4) transfer or reciprocity of licensure between states, (5) revocation of license, (6) penalty for practicing without a license, and (7) regulation of study programs offered nurses.

DEFINITION OF NURSING

The model definition of nursing suggested by the American Nurses' Association in 1955 and 1970 is modified to some degree in the state acts. The new definitions of nursing encompass the scope of nursing practice and define the expanded role of nursing today.

In the state of Washington the practice of nursing means

. . . the performance of acts requiring substantial specialized knowledge, judgement and skill based upon the principles of the biological, physiological, behavioral and sociological sciences in either:
(1) The observation, assessment, diagnosis, care or counsel, and health teaching of the ill, injured or infirm, or in the maintenance of health or prevention of illness of others.
(2) The performance of such additional acts requiring education and training and which are recognized jointly by the medical and nursing professions as proper to be performed by nurses licensed under this chapter and which shall be authorized by the Board of Nursing through its rules and regulations.
(3) The administration, supervision, delegation and evaluation of nursing practice: PROVIDED HOWEVER, That nothing herein shall affect the authority of any hospital, hospital district, medical clinic or office, concerning its administration and supervision.
(4) The teaching of nursing.
(5) The executing of medical regimen as prescribed by a licensed physician, osteopathic physician, dentist, or chiropodist [6].

For a comparison, in the state of California the practice of professional nursing is defined as

. . .those functions helping people cope with difficulties in daily living which are associated with their actual or potential health or illness problems or the treatment thereof which require a substantial amount of scientific knowledge or technical skill, and includes all of the following:
(a) Direct and indirect patient care services that insure the safety, comfort, personal hygiene, and protection of patients; and the performance of disease prevention and restorative measures.
(b) Direct and indirect patient care services, including, but not limited to, the administration of medications and therapeutic agents, necessary to implement a treatment, disease prevention, or rehabilitative regimen prescribed by a physician, dentist, or podiatrist.
(c) The performance, according to standardized procedures, of basic health care, testing, and prevention procedures, including, but not limited to, skin tests, immunization techniques, and the withdrawal of human blood from veins and arteries.

(d) Observation of signs and symptoms of illness, reactions to treatment, general behavior, or general physical condition, and (1) determination of whether such signs, symptoms, reactions, behavior, or general appearance exhibit abnormal characteristics; and (2) implementation, based on observed abnormalities, of appropriate reporting, or referral, or standardized procedures, or changes in treatment regimen in accordance with standardized procedures, or the initiation of emergency procedures.

"Standardized procedures," as used in this section, means either of the following:

(1) Policies and protocols developed by a health facility licensed pursuant to Chapter 2 (commencing with Section 1250) of Division 2 of the Health and Safety Code through collaboration among administrators and health professionals including physicians and nurses;

(2) Policies and protocols developed through collaboration among administrators and health professionals, including physicians and nurses, by an organized health care system which is not a health facility licensed pursuant to Chapter 2 (commencing with Section 1250) of of Division 2 of the Health and Safety Code. Such policies and protocols shall be subject to any guidelines for standardized procedures which the Board of Medical Examiners and the Board of Nursing Education and Nurse Registration may jointly promulgate; and if promulgated shall be administered by the Board of Nursing Education and Nurse Registration.

Nothing in this section shall be construed to require approval of standardized procedures by the Board of Medical Examiners or the Board of Nursing Education and Nurse Registration [7].

The National League for Nursing and the American Nurses' Association acknowledge that all registered nurses who have graduated from an approved Bachelor of Science in Nursing program are qualified to be nurse practitioners and provide primary health care. The duties that they could perform in a nursing home setting include

(1) obtaining a health history
(2) assessing health-illness status
(3) entering an individual in a health care system
(4) sustaining and supporting individuals who are impaired, infirm, ill, and undergoing programs of diagnosis and therapy
(5) managing a medical care regime for acute and chronically ill patients within established standing orders
(6) assisting individuals in regaining their health
(7) teaching and counseling individuals about health and illness
(8) counseling and supporting individuals and families with respect to the aging and dying process
(9) supervising nursing assistants [8]

Most states have a definition of the practice of professional nursing similar to the American Nurses' Association's 1955 model, including a statement to the effect that the practice of professional nursing ". . . shall not be deemed to include acts of diagnosis or prescription of therapeutic or corrective measures'' [9]. There remains the question of whether or not nurses in intensive care units and coronary care units acting on standing orders, but frequently independent of physician supervision, can assume they are practicing legally within the nurse practice acts. There is a dearth of case law passing on the legality of the nurse's status when she performs quasi-medical functions pursuant to standing orders from the physician. We must assume that, with the current interest in the expanded role of the nurse, it will not be long before the courts are forced to come to grips with this problem. The law involving the status of professional nurses is in a rapidly evolving state. This area, in particular, is a vacuum crying to be filled.

Nurses, working in these specialized settings, in states with nurse practice acts that specifically exclude acts of medical diagnosis or treatment are relying on the fact that they are acting in an emergency situation that would be considered an exception to the rule prohibiting them from making a medical diagnosis or prescribing medical therapeutic measures. Can an emergency exception apply when a nurse is employed by an institution to give daily care in a unit in which an emergency is the rule and not the exception? We believe that the legislation of the future must provide more specific guidelines in this area.

The state of California appears to have provided for an orderly transfer of medical responsibilities to actual nursing practice by providing for the following:

. . .determination of whether such signs, symptoms, reactions, behavior, or general appearance exhibit abnormal characteristics; and implementation based on observed abnormalities, of appropriate reporting, or referral or standardized procedures or changes in treatment regime in accordance with standardized procedures, or the initiation of emergency procedures [7].

Standardized procedures are futher defined as meaning

. . .policies and protocols developed by a health facility . . . policies and protocols developed . . . through collaboration among administrators and health professionals including physicians and nurses. . . . Such policies and protocols shall be subject to any guidelines for standardized procedures which the Board of Medical Examiners and the Board of Nursing Education and Nurse Registration may jointly promulgate; and if promulgated shall be administered by the Board of Nursing Education and Nurse Registration [7].

The double usage of the word *diagnosis* for medical diagnosis and diagnosis by nurses in twenty-one states adds to the confusion. Prior statutory and judicial decisions in these states define diagnosis as "the asserting of a disease or ailment by the symptoms.'' The nurse's responsibility is only to make a judgment regarding the gravity of the symptoms and to act under the direction of the physician. These states have not within their acts defined the meaning of diagnosis by nurses [10]. Pennsylvania, on the other hand, defines diagnosis by nurses as ''. . .that identification of and a discrimination between physical and psychological signs and symptoms essential to effective execution and management of a nursing regime'' [17]. In this era of expanded health care services, it is essential that uncertainties be eliminated.

In 1974, the first attempt was made to compile a list of nursing diagnoses [11].

Alterations in faith (in oneself, in others, in God)
Altered relationships with self and others
Altered self-concept
Anxiety
Body fluids, depletion of
Bowel function, irregular
Cognitive functioning, alteration in the level of
Comfort level, alterations in
Confusion (disorientation)
Deprivation
Digestion, impairment of
Family's adjustment to illness, impairment of
Family process, inadequate
Fear
Grieving
Lack of understanding
Level of consciousness, alterations in
Malnutrition
Manipulation
Mobility, impaired
Motor incoordination
Non-compliance
Pain
Regulatory function of the skin, impairment of
Respiration, impairment of
Respiratory distress
Self-care activities, altered ability to perform
Sensory disturbances
Skin integrity, impairment of
Sleep and rest pattern, ineffective
Susceptibility to hazards
Thought process, impaired
Urinary elimination, impairment of
Verbal communication, impairment of

The process of inclusion and exclusion of diagnostic terms involves decisions. At present there is no statement of the criteria for inclusion or exclusion though some might be inferred. Some labels were proposals which are not developed well enough for us to decide whether they should be included or eliminated. These diagnoses were depression, developmental lag, jaundice, sexuality problems, stress, and suicide-potential. Several other labels were discussed, accepted as preliminary, and then discarded. Dependent personality and drug dependence, for example were identified and then discarded.*

A list of nursing diagnoses accepted within the profession would allow nurses to share a common language, as medical diagnoses allow physicians to communicate. Otitis media and rheumatoid arthritis, for example, are two medical diagnoses that suggest the presence of well-known signs and symptoms. An all-inclusive list of nursing diagnoses would define the practice of nursing and would help to indicate where nursing research is needed.

COMPOSITION AND RESPONSIBILITY OF THE STATE BOARD OF NURSING

The composition of the state board of nursing in Pennsylvania (State Board of Nurse Examiners) is not defined by the Professional Nursing Law of Pennsylvania. It is provided for by a statute that, not unlike those in other states, calls for a board made up of a state official and five registered nurses appointed by the governor from a list submitted by the Pennsylvania Nurses' Association. The State Board of Nurse Examiners in Pennsylvania makes rulings affecting licensed practical nurses (LPNs) as well as registered nurses (RNs) [12]. As of March, 1974, 31 states have added LPNs and other health personnel to their state boards of nurse examiners [13]. If the nursing profession is to serve the public's health needs, it seems logical to appoint consumers to serve on nurse licensing boards. At present seven states have consumer representation [13].

The National League for Nursing, in its *Position Statement on Nursing Licensure,* states that the policy decisions regarding the practice of nursing require nursing expertise and should continue to be made by a separate nursing licensure board composed of a majority of RNs. The National League for Nursing feels that consumers should be appointed to serve on nurse licensing boards and that LPNs should be appointed to serve on nurse licensing boards since the LPN is required by law in most states to work under the supervision of an RN and is given her nursing instruction by an RN [14]. In addition, the nurse practice acts of many states govern the licensure of both RNs and LPNs. Many nurses feel that they alone should control the education and practice of nurses. We feel that state boards of nursing would benefit from representation of other health personnel and of the public that the nursing profession serves; however,

* Coypright February 1974, The American Journal of Nursing Company. Reproduced with permission from the *American Journal of Nursing*, Vol. 74, No. 2.

since RNs bear the major responsibility for their own profession, the majority of board representation should remain professional nurses.

LICENSURE
Requirements for Licensure
In all states, an application for licensure must be filed. Applicants are required to have successfully completed a state-approved nursing education program. Fees for examination, reexamination, and renewal of licensure are required. Physical and mental health, age, citizenship, and moral character are issues in some states. The states may set a time limit in which the licensure examination must be taken by the graduate nurse. For 25 years the state nursing licensing boards have been using the national, standardized licensing examination. The licensure requirements for professional nurses in title 45, chapter 11, section 11-26 of the state of New Jersey stipulate the following:

(a) Qualifications of applicants. An applicant for a license to practice professional nursing shall submit to the board evidence in such form as the board may prescribe that said applicant: (1) has attained his or her eighteenth birthday; (2) is of good moral character, is not a habitual user of drugs and has never been convicted or has not pleaded nolo contendere, non vult contendere or non vult to an indictment, information or complaint alleging a violation of any Federal or State law relating to narcotic drugs; (3) holds a diploma from an accredited 4-year high school or the equivalent thereof as determined by the New Jersey State Department of Education; (4) has completed a course of professional nursing study in an accredited school of professional nursing as defined by the board and holds a diploma therefrom.
Notwithstanding anything herein contained, any person who possesses the educational and school of professional nursing qualifications for registration required by the law of this State at the time of his or her graduation from an accredited school of professional nursing shall be deemed to possess the qualifications (3) and (4) prescribed hereinabove in this subsection.
Notwithstanding anything herein contained, any person who shall have qualifications (1) and (2) and shall have graduated from a school of professional nursing, which need not be an accredited school, shall be deemed to have qualifications (3) and (4) upon complying with such reasonable requirements as to high school and school of nursing studies and training as the board may prescribe; provided, however, that such person shall make application in form prescribed by the board within 1 year from the effective date of this act and shall satisfactorily complete such reasonable requirements and successfully pass the examinations, which examinations shall be limited to subject matters in the curriculum required by the board at the time of the applicant's graduation, provided for in subsection b. hereof, within 2 years after the date of the filing of such applicant.

(b) License.
  (1) By examination. The applicant shall be required to pass a written examination in such subjects as the board may determine, which examination may be supplemented by an oral or practical examination or both. Upon successfully passing such examinations the applicant shall be licensed by the board to practice professional nursing.
  (2) By endorsement without examination. The board may issue a license to practice professional nursing without examination to an applicant who has been duly licensed or registered as a registered or professional nurse by examination or by original waiver under the laws of another State, territory or possession of the United States, or the District of Columbia, or any foreign country, if in the opinion of the board the applicant has the qualifications required by this act for the licensing of professional nurses, or equivalent qualifications.
(c) Fees. An applicant for a license by examination shall pay to the board at the time of application a fee of $25.00 and at the time of each application for reexamination a fee of $20.00. An applicant for a license without examination shall pay to the board at the time of application a fee of $15.00.
(d) Nurses registered under a previous law. Any person who on the effective date of this act holds a subsisting certificate of registration as a registered nurse issued pursuant to the provisions of the act repealed by section 22 of this act shall be deemed to be licensed as a professional nurse under this act during the calendar year in which this act shall take effect, and such person and any person who heretofore held a certificate of registration under said act hereby repealed as aforesaid shall be entitled to a renewal of such license as in the case of professional nurses licensed originally under this act.
(e) Title and abbreviations used by licensee. Any person who holds a license to practice professional nursing under this act shall during the effective period of such license be entitled to use the title "Registered Nurse" and the abbreviation "R.N." The effective period of a license or a renewal thereof shall commence on the date of issuance and shall terminate at the end of the calendar year in which it is issued, and shall not include any period of suspension ordered by the board as hereinafter provided [15].

In a 1971 report on licensure, the Department of Health, Education, and Welfare complimented the nursing profession for standardizing proficiency in nursing care and providing for geographic mobility within the profession [14]. Whereas each state has the right to establish what is considered a passing score on the State Board Test Poll Examination for professional nurses, there is a current consensus that the score of 350 of 800 possible points is considered passing. The National League for Nursing supports mandatory licensure for RNs and LPNs [14].

Most nurse practice acts today are considered mandatory laws. However, they necessarily include many exceptions, for example, family members, neighbors, and domestics, limiting the actual control of personnel giving health-related care. The necessity for the exemptions listed in nursing practice acts is obvious; however, the proliferation of new types of health workers, such as physicians' assistants, has made many doubt the effectiveness of mandatory professional licensure. New York's Nurse Practice Act, section 6907, defines the following exemptions:

(1)   This article shall not be construed:
   (a)   As prohibiting the care of the sick by any person, provided such person is employed primarily in a domestic capacity and does not hold himself or herself out, or accept employment as a person registered to practice nursing under the provision of this article, or as preventing any person from the domestic administration of family remedies or the furnishing of nursing assistance in case of an emergency;
   (b)   As including services given by attendants in institutions under the jurisdiction of or subject to the visitation of the state department of mental hygiene if adequate medical and nursing supervision is provided;
   (c)   As prohibiting such performance of nursing service by students enrolled in registered schools or programs as may be incidental to their course of study;
   (d)   As prohibiting or preventing the practice of nursing in this state by any legally qualified nurse or practical nurse of another state, province, or country whose engagement requires him or her to accompany and care for a patient temporarily residing in this state during the period of such engagement provided such person does not represent or hold himself or herself out as a nurse or practical nurse registered to practice in this state;
   (e)   As prohibiting or preventing the practice of nursing in this state during an emergency or disaster by any legally qualified nurse or practical nurse of another state, province, or country who may be recruited by the American National Red Cross or pursuant to authority vested in the state civil defense commission for such emergency or disaster service, provided such person does not represent or hold himself or herself out as a nurse or practical nurse registered to practice in this state;
   (f)   As prohibiting or preventing the practice of nursing in this state, in obedience to the requirements of the laws of the United States, by any commissioned nurse officer in the armed forces of the United States or by any nurse employed in the United States veterans administration or United States public health service while engaged in the performance of the actual duties prescribed for him or her under the United States statutes, provided such person does not represent or hold himself or herself out as a nurse registered to practice in this state; or
   (g)   As prohibiting the care of the sick when done in connection with the practice of the religious tenets of any church [16].

Transfer or Reciprocity of Licensure Between States
The reciprocity of nursing licensure between states is greatly aided by the

National Standardized Licensing Examination spoken of previously. A nurse asking for endorsement for licensure in a state in which she has not been previously licensed must make application to the state and is generally required to produce evidence of having passed an educational course equivalent in requirements to that of the state in which licensure is being requested. In some states the additional requirements of age, citizenship, physical and mental health, and good moral character must be met.

Revocation of a License

Suspension or revocation of a license in the State of Pennsylvania is dealt with in section 14 of the Professional Nursing Law:

The Board may suspend or revoke any license in any case where the Board shall find that—

(1) The licensee is on repeated occasions negligent or incompetent in the practice of professional nursing.

(2) The licensee is unable to practice professional nursing with reasonable skill and safety to patients by reason of mental or physical illness or condition or physiological or psychological dependence upon alcohol, hallucinogenic or narcotic drugs or other drugs which tend to impair judgment or coordination, so long as such dependence shall continue. In enforcing this clause (2), the Board shall, upon probable cause, have authority to compel a licensee to submit to a mental or physical examination as designated by it. After notice, hearing, adjudication and appeal as provided for in section 15, failure of a licensee to submit to such examination when directed shall constitute an admission of the allegations against him unless failure is due to circumstances beyond his control, consequent upon which a default and final order may be entered without the taking of testimony or presentation of evidence. A licensee affected under this paragraph shall at reasonable intervals be afforded an opportunity to demonstrate that he can resume a competent practice of professional nursing with reasonable skill and safety to patients.

(3) The licensee has willfully or repeatedly violated any of the provisions of this act or of the regulations of the Board.

(4) The licensee has committed fraud or deceit in the practice of nursing, or in securing his or her admission to such practice.

(5) The licensee has been convicted, or has pleaded guilty, or entered a plea of nolo contendere, or has been found guilty by a judge or jury, of a felony in the courts of this Commonwealth or any other state, territory or country.

(6) The licensee has his license suspended or revoked in another state, territory or country [17].

Suspension in a majority of the states is based on the protection of the public from a nurse who is unable to function competently due to alcohol usage, drug addiction, lack of mental or physical well-being, or failure to abide by the standards and requirements of the nurse practice act of her particular state.

Penalty for Practicing Without a License
In addition to monitoring the practice of nursing within the state, most nurse practice acts include a provision for penalties for practicing nursing without a license. Section 13 of the Professional Nursing Law of Pennsylvania stipulates fines and periods of imprisonment for violating the law or practicing nursing without a license.

Any person, or the responsible officers or employees of any corporation, copartnership, institution or association violating any of the provision of this act, shall, upon summary conviction thereof, be sentenced to pay a fine of three hundred dollars ($300); and in default of the payment of such fine and costs, to undergo imprisonment for a period of ninety (90) days, unless nonpayment of said fine is shown by affidavit made by the defendant to the court, to be the result of the defendant's indigency [17].

There is a wide variety of penalties throughout the country, and fines range from $5 to hundreds of dollars with or without a period of imprisonment.

REGULATION OF STUDY PROGRAMS OFFERED NURSES

By mandating that applicants for licensure must have completed a state approved program of nursing education, state nurse practice acts regulate study programs in nursing within the state. New Jersey's nursing act, section 11-33, stipulates the requirements for a school of professional nursing:

   (a) Application for accreditation. Any person, partnership, association, corporation or public educational institution desiring to conduct a school of professional nursing shall submit to the board evidence in such form as the board may require that the applicant: (1) is equipped to give the course of instruction and practice set forth in the curriculum prescribed by the board, part of which instruction and practice may, with the approval of the board, be given by arrangement with one or more agencies or institutions approved by the board for that purpose; (2) is affiliated with a hospital of such size and facilities as the board may prescribe; (3) meets such other standards and requirements as the board may prescribe. In any case other than an application by a public educational institution the board may require evidence of good moral character of all persons directly or indirectly interested in the operation of such school. Upon approval of the application the board shall issue a certificate of accreditation, which may be conditional during the first year.

   (b) Rights and obligations of holders of certificates of accreditation. The holder of a certificate of accreditation shall have the right during the effective period of the certificate of accreditation to conduct a school of professional nursing. The effective period of such certificate or a renewal thereof shall commence on the date of issuance and shall terminate at the end of the fiscal year, July first to June thirtieth, in which it is issued, and shall not include any period of suspension ordered by the board as hereinafter provided. An accredited school of professional nursing shall admit as students only persons possessing the preliminary educational requirements set forth in section four hereof, shall abide by and conform to the curriculum and standards of operation prescribed from time to time by the board, shall make such reports to the board as the board may require, and shall submit to such investigations by representatives of the board as the board may require [15].

Section 6.2 of Pennsylvania's nursing law particularly deals with the board's responsibility of preparing lists of all programs approved by the state for public distribution [17]. In this aspect of the nursing laws, as in other areas of the acts, when the laws are written in broad terms, it is the responsibility of the state boards to interpret and regulate nursing practice. In most states an effort has been made to write the nurse practice acts in broad terms so that the state boards can keep in tune with society's changing needs for nursing services; for example, what should be the curriculum of a state-approved nursing program in 1980? New legislation is purposely written to be adapted for the present and the future. The field of nursing, the allied health professions, the lay public, and the court system will all have roles in implementing this broad legislation.

All nurse practice acts provide for the state boards to have the right to promulgate any rules or regulations that are needed to carry out the acts. Pennsylvania had five nursing regulations that were promulgated under the authority of the Professional Nurse Law. These regulations dealt with administration and withdrawal of intravenous fluids; external cardiac resuscitation and artificial respiration; administration of drugs; use of monitoring, defibrillating, and resuscitating equipment; and administration of anesthesia. As an example, the regulation dealing with administration of drugs states

The State Board of Nurse Examiners, under the authority of the Act of May 22, 1951 (P.L. 317) known as "The Professional Nurse Law," establishes that administering to a patient a drug ordered for that patient by a licensed doctor of medicine, osteopathy or dentistry in the dosage prescribed, is a procedure within the scope of the practice of professional nursing as it is defined in the Act.
A licensed registered nurse, responsible for administering a drug, may supervise a person other than a licensed registered nurse in the administration of the drug if, within the meaning of Sub-section 7, Section IV of the Act, administering the drug is an auxiliary service necessary for the support of nursing service or is a minor nursing service and if, in the judgment of the licensed registered nurse, the person administering the drug is competent to perform this procedure [18].

State regulations are available by writing to the state board of nursing of one's particular state.

Continuing education is a necessary responsibility of any professional group. Until the recent surge in nursing legislation, the nurse licensure laws in force were enacted prior to the technological revolution in health care and did not provide for the possibility that a nurse's professional skills might become obsolete. Until recent years, all nursing licensure laws required one examination that was taken on completion of a course of nursing study. However, the Department of Health, Education, and Welfare now considers that there is no way one test can adequately protect the public [19]. The dissension within the nursing profession does not appear to be over the need for nurses to continually educate themselves, but rather, whether this continuing education should be mandatory. The National League for Nursing in a position statement titled *NLN's Role in Continuing Education, February 1974,* recommends that "A continuing education requirement for the relicensure of nurses should be carefully planned and gradually implemented" [20].

There is a question in the minds of many nurses as to whether the imposition of mandatory continuing education for nurses detracts from the status of the profession. This is particularly true at a time when nursing is still striving to overcome its subordinate position to the medical profession, which in most states does not have mandatory continuing-education requirements. Although other professions have, in general, been unwilling to accept the responsibility and inconvenience of mandatory continuing education, we believe that nursing has a responsibility to the public to implement such a program. In addition to enhancing the status of nursing as a profession, mandatory continuing education, at the initiative of nurses' themselves, will demonstrate both foresight and responsibility. Some state nurses' associations are presently providing both certification and record keeping for voluntary continuing education programs. The state of California has already passed mandatory legislation for continuing education for nurses [7]. The original health bill in the state of Pennsylvania contained a provision for continuing education, but this was omitted in the final act [21]. The American Nurses' Association has supported voluntary continuing-education programs [22].

If the legislatures find it necessary to pass mandatory continuing-education laws in order to provide protection for the public, many nurses will be disheartened by the public's lack of faith in the ethical standards of the nursing profession. This is but one more case in which the consumer movement is placing health professionals in the same defensive posture as merchants and manufacturers.

In numerous reports from the Department of Health, Education, and Welfare, mandatory continuing education for all health professionals has been recommended. With an eye toward the future and an ear to the past, it appears evident that federal legislation will press for continuing education by controlling federal funding. State boards should begin to study how to make continuing education available and enforceable within their own states.

Most of the new nurse practice acts now include a legal commitment to health teaching and health counseling. Most baccalaureate curricula have included the principles of learning and teaching and the opportunity to practice both in a clinical setting. It is important that all programs preparing registered nurses include the training necessary to produce a nurse who is a competent health educator. If nurses are to be the principal health educators of the public, they must have the knowledge, ability, and motivation to teach. They must be able to document and to evaluate the health education they are giving. This is indeed an exciting challenge for nurses.

With all of the similarities among the new nursing laws throughout the country, there still remains a great deal that is unique to each state law. It is the professional's responsibility to be familiar with the nurse practice act of the state in which she or he practices. If the reader would like a copy of his or her nursing law, we suggest writing either to local state legislators or to the state board of nursing. It is a good idea to inform a state legislator of the presence of concerned nurses in his constituency. In spite of the size of its membership, the nursing profession is just beginning to make use of its political muscle.

If you plan to write your state legislator asking for an act, why not make it the first of many letters expressing both your civic and your professional interest in state legislation.

Bona fide criticism of the present individual nurse licensure laws has led some to suggest institutional licensure for health workers as a solution. This would make the employing institution or agency responsible for the health services rendered, rather than holding the professional nurses individually responsible for the quality of nursing care. Institutional licensure would make the institution or agency responsible for defining the nursing practice. In a major position statement on nursing licensure, the National League for Nursing stated: "The institution would have the power which could be abused, to place health professionals in positions where needed, regardless of the employee's education or certification" [14]. The reduced costs predicted by those in favor of institutional licensure must be expected to be gained by employing fewer professionals and allowing cheaper, less qualified workers to give health care. At present, the cost of individual licensure in all states is borne by the individual applying for a license or for license renewal. The cost of institutional licensure in most states is paid through public funding or tax dollars. The financial burden of institutional licensure, in addition to calling for increased public funding, would call for additional institution or agency costs for the increased legal liability being borne by the employing agency rather than the individual. Nursing licensure laws presently are not perfect. The professional nurse should remain individually accountable for the acts she performs within the scope of her professional service. No professional should be able to claim "no fault." Rather than abandoning the present position of individual licensure, and turning to an uncertain policy of institutional licensure, the individual nurse licensure procedure should be strengthened. This could be accomplished by maintaining a national standardized licensing examination, by appointing consumers and licensed practical nurses to serve on nurse licensing boards, and by planning and gradually implementing continuing-education requirements for relicensure. We believe that institutional licensure would derogate from the status of nursing as a learned profession and would also detract from the quality of nursing care delivered to the public.

REFERENCES

1. Kipling, Rudyard. *The ladies*, stanza 8.
2. American Nurses' Association. *1973 legislative survey*. Kansas City, Missouri, June, 1973.
3. American Nurses' Association. *Memo to executive director of state nurses' associations and state boards of nursing*. Kansas City, Missouri, April 3, 1970.
4. Herbert, C. L. *Rules and regulations for Catoosa Hospital*. Griffin, Georgia, 1863. (Courtesy of the Museum of the Confederacy, Richmond, Virginia.)
5. Beletz, Elaine E. Is nursing's public image up to date? *Nurs. Outlook* 22:432, 1974.
6. Title 18, Washington Code, Section 18.88.050.
7. State of California. *Business and professional code*, Section 2725.
8. Pennsylvania League for Nursing. *News bulletin* (Harrisburg), October, 1975, p. 11.
9. State of Colorado, Professional Nursing Practice Act.
10. Brug, Charles D., et al. Acts of diagnosis of nurses and the Colorado Professional Nursing Act. *Denver Law J.* 45:470, 1968.
11. Grebbie, Christine, et al. Classifying nursing diagnoses. *Am. J. Nurs.* 75:252, 1975.
12. Pennsylvania Code Annotated, Title 71, section 128.
13. Kelly, Lucy Young. Nursing practice acts. *Am. J. Nurs.* 74:1317, 1974.
14. National League for Nursing. *Position statement of nursing licensure*. New York, February, 1975.
15. New Jersey Code Annotated, Title 45, chapter 11: Nurses.
16. New York Code Annotated, Title 8, article 139: Nursing.
17. Pennsylvania Public Law 151. July 3, 1974.

18. Nursing Regulation No. 3, promulgated under the act of May 22, 1951 Pennsylvania Public Law 317: Administration of Drugs.
19. U.S. Department of Health, Education, and Welfare. *Report of the Secretary's commission on medical malpractice.* Washington, D.C.: DHEW, January 16, 1973.
20. National League for Nursing. *NLN's role in continuing education.* New York, February, 1974.
21. The General Assembly of Pennsylvania, House Bill No. 29, Session of 1973, p. 13.
22. American Nurses' Association. *Statement on continuing education.* Kansas City, Missouri, 1974.

8. CONSUMERISM
AND ACCOUNTABILITY

The American consumer revolution began when Theodore Roosevelt signed the first Pure Food and Drug Act on June 30, 1906. Dr. H. W. Wiley, Director of the Department of Agriculture, instigated the first case prosecuted under the Pure Food and Drug Act of 1906. It was against a medication patented as Cufurhedaeke Brane-Fude. The judge ruled that this product should be taken off the market and stated, "This law was passed not to protect experts especially, not to protect scientific men who know the meaning and value of drugs, but for the purpose of protecting citizens." [1]

John F. Kennedy, while campaigning for the presidency, stated, "The consumer is the only man in our economy without a high-powered lobbyist. I intend to be that lobbyist." About one year after Kennedy was elected, he set forth what he called the "Consumer Bill of Rights." This bill of rights included

(1) The right to safety—to be protected against the marketing of goods which are hazardous to health or life.
(2) The right to be informed—to be protected against fraudulent, deceitful, or grossly misleading information, advertising, labeling, or other practices, and to be given the facts needed to make an informed choice.
(3) The right to choose—to be assured, wherever possible, access to a variety of products and services at competitive prices; and in those industries where competition is not workable and government regulation is substituted, an assurance of satisfactory quality and service at fair prices.
(4) The right to be heard—to be assured that consumer interest will receive full and sympathetic consideration in the formulation of government policy, and fair and expeditious treatment in its administrative tribunals [2].

Kennedy wished to expand the role of the federal government in protecting the consumer. He urged Congress to help him by providing more funding. When the Better Business Bureau joined the consumer revolution, the stage was set for Ralph Nader. The Better Business Bureau reported that 50 percent of the entire population believed all advertising to be a batch of lies. This meant that the American corporation was wasting 50 cents on every dollar it spent in advertising. The Better Business Bureau requested the corporations to give to the bureau one-quarter of 1 percent of the corporations' national advertising budget. The Better Business Bureau

83

promised to spend this one-quarter of 1 percent attempting to clean up the marketplace so the remaining 99 percent spent in advertising would prove to be more effective [3].

The first reaction by business to legislation which is aimed at solving legitimate consumer complaints is to deny the existence of a consumer problem. Only since industry has been subject to consumer-oriented legislation have corporations moved to resolve their consumer problems.

The health professions, like the corporations, have failed to monitor themselves. The general public, being better educated today than it has been in the past, is more informed in the areas of health and illness. The lay public has been exposed to the most complex medical and nursing problems and terminology through newspapers, magazines, and television. Having been so exposed, the public feels more comfortable in its communications with health professionals. The health care consumer is no longer a captive in a world he does not understand. Health care recipients are recognized as consumers of health services. They are able to share in the decisions about their health care and to assume responsibility for their health. They are being encouraged to know the seven signs of cancer, to have a yearly physical, to have their blood pressure checked regularly, to do a monthly breast examination, and to buy drugs by their generic names rather than their trade names when possible.

The federal and state governments have become the advocates of the individual's right to quality health care through the stringent requirements they place on institutions and agencies that receive government funding. Only when the health agencies and health professionals have been required by law to acknowledge their responsibility to the health consumer will they have admitted the existence of consumer problems and take action to resolve these problems. It is this type of consumer-oriented legislation that has resulted in a new outlook for health care institutions. Citizen board members have been appointed as community advocates to hospital and agency boards. Professional standards review organizations are being developed. Quality assurance committees performing medical and nursing audits are becoming more common. Quality control specialists are being hired by health institutions and agencies in an attempt to apply industrial type controls to the health services they offer.

Within the last ten years, interest in consumerism, especially as it relates to the health care professions, has increased tremendously. Nurses, physicians, dentists, and health care facilities are bombarded with assaults in the courts, the legislatures, and the media for failure to maintain adequate quality control in health care delivery. Lack of accountability is a battle cry of consumer advocates in the health care field. Is contemporary society guilty of overkill? Every movement, no matter how worthwhile its goals, can become counterproductive under the leadership of zealots who are, so to speak, willing to cut off their noses to spite their faces. While it is true that some health care professionals, including nurses, have abused the independence and trust they enjoy, it is also true that excessive regimentation and harassment may engender an attitude among them that is extremely detrimental to good health care delivery. An example with which all practicing nurses are familiar is the excessive testing and conservatism now being practiced by physicians who are almost paranoid in their fear of malpractice suits. Are the patients really getting a better deal? We think that this is an area where there must be a balancing of the various interests involved. Certainly there has been an irritating tendency toward elitism on the part of some physicians, and to a lesser degree on the part of some hospital administrators and nurses. This has had a certain backlash in the legitimate demands of the consumer movement for better health care delivery. Some of this backlash is evidenced in excessive awards in malpractice cases that are out of all proportion to the injuries received by claimants.

Anyone who places himself in an ivory tower invites the public to attempt to pull him down. The nursing profession, the medical profession, and other health care professions have an obligation to provide more accountability and better quality control than they have in the past.

Consumer demands, frequently referred to as rights, affect the nursing profession in many ways in its dealings with patients and with nursing students. The rights accorded nurses and women in general are also an important factor in the development of the nursing profession.

PATIENT RIGHTS

The health care consumer is more particularly referred to as the patient. The nursing profession today is constantly being challenged to join the consumer, or to become the patient's advocate. Once a patient or client has entered the health care system, it is considered a nursing function to coordinate the care he or she receives. In order for the nurse to perform this service, she must be familiar with what care, planning, and evaluation the patient is eligible to receive. The American Hospital Association, in November of 1972, adopted a statement of 12 principles which became known as the *Patient's Bill of Rights* [5]:

(1) The patient has the right to considerate and respectful care.
(2) The patient has the right to obtain from his physician complete current information concerning his diagnosis, treatment, and prognosis in terms the patient can be reasonably expected to understand.
(3) The patient has the right to receive from his physician information necessary to give informed consent prior to the start of any procedure and/or treatment. . .Where medically significant alternatives for care or treatment exist, or when the patient requests information con-

cerning medical alternatives, the patient has the right to such information (and) to know the name of the person responsible for the procedures and/or treatment.

(4) The patient has the right to refuse treatment to the extent permitted by law, and to be informed of the medical consequences of his action.

(5) The patient has the right to every consideration of his privacy concerning his own medical care program.

(6) The patient has the right to expect that all communications and records pertaining to his care should be treated as confidential.

(7) The patient has the right to expect that within its capacity a hospital must make reasonable response to the request of a patient for services.

(8) The patient has the right to obtain information as to any relationship of his hospital to other health care and educational institutions insofar as his care in concerned. . .(and) any professional relationships among individuals, by name, who are treating him.

(9) The patient has the right to be advised if the hospital proposes to engage in or perform human experimentation affecting his care or treatment. . .(and) has the right to refuse to participate.

(10) The patient has the right to expect reasonable continuity of care.

(11) The patient has the right to examine and receive an explanation of his bill regardless of source of payment.

(12) The patient has the right to know what hospital rules and regulations apply to his conduct as a patient.*

In 1973, the state of Minnesota became the first state to require "That the interest of patients be protected by a patient bill of rights. . ." [6]. The Minnesota law further requires that this bill of rights be posted in a conspicuous public place within the institution and that each patient or resident receive a copy. The American Hospital Association's *Patient's Bill of Rights* only reiterates what have already been considered both the legal and the ethical responsiblities of hospitals and health professionals. The Minnesota law is the first such law to be passed by a state legislature; however, numerous hospitals throughout the country have themselves been adopting a patient's bill of rights. This is as it should be, for it is the institution or agency which must provide personnel in the numbers required and which must allot the time and the inservice education necessary for the personnel to meet all of the patients' rights and needs.

We have acknowledged the controversy of legal and ethical definitions of death including an entire chapter on the subject (Chap. 11). In 1974, at a workshop titled "The Terminally Ill Patient and the Helping Person," sponsored by the Southwestern Michigan Inservice Educational Council, a bill of rights was created entitled *The Dying Person's Bill of Rights* [7].

I have the right to be treated as a living human being until I die.
I have the right to maintain a sense of hopefulness, however changing its focus may be.

*Reprinted with the permission of the American Hospital Association.

I have the right to be cared for by those who can maintain a sense of hopefulness, however changing this might be.

I have the right to express my feelings and emotions about my approaching death in my own way.

I have the right to participate in decisions concerning my care.

I have the right to expect continuing medical and nursing attention even though "cure" goals must be changed to "comfort" goals.

I have the right not to die alone.

I have the right to be free from pain.

I have the right to have my questions answered honestly.

I have the right not to be deceived.

I have the right to have help from and for my family in accepting my death.

I have the right to die in peace and dignity.

I have the right to retain my individuality and not be judged for my decisions which may be contrary to beliefs of others.

I have the right to discuss and enlarge my religious and/or spiritual experiences, whatever these may mean to others.

I have the right to expect that the sanctity of the human body will be respected after death.

I have the right to be cared for by caring, sensitive, knowledgeable people who will attempt to understand my needs and will be able to gain some satisfaction in helping me face my death.*

An involuntarily hospitalized mental patient who is not deemed dangerous to himself or others may only be receiving custodial care. If he is capable of living in the community safely, he has been returned his constitutional right to liberty, or the right to be released from the hospital, by a 1975 United States Supreme Court decision, *O'Connor v. Donaldson* [8]. The law will affect only patients fitting the Donaldson criteria, that is, they will have to have been: (1) involuntarily committed, (2) receiving only custodial care, (3) not dangerous to themselves or others, and (4) capable of surviving safely in the community, alone or with help of family or friends. The various state courts will interpret this decision and make rulings regarding varying categories of patients. The numerous state mental health associations are looking to the decision, which holds that: "A state cannot constitutionally confine *without more* a nondangerous individual. . ." (emphasis added), and are hoping to secure an interpretation of *without more* to mean without more than custodial care. This type of interpretation could define as a constitutional right treatment for the mentally ill that would realistically enable them to be cured of their mental disorders.

It is obvious that every patient could have a bill of rights written expressing his individual requirements. The nursing profession has attempted to do this in individualized nursing care plans. The American Nurses'

Association has more recently attempted to do this by establishing Standards of Nursing Practice. This obligation to set standards for the nursing profession and to assist nurses with implementation of these standards was adopted by the American Nurses' Association Board of Directors and endorsed by the 1974 convention delegates as their first priority for the 1974-1976 biennium.

STUDENTS' RIGHTS

Nurses employed as nursing educators within teaching institutions must be aware of a new accountability being placed on education. The nursing student is considered to be a consumer today, and the product she is buying is her education. She differs from other consumers in that she is investing not only her money but also a lot of herself and her time. In order for a nursing student to acquire the necessary skills from her education, she must have ability and commitment. The licensure requirements help protect the public against unqualified practitioners. In nursing, the students are protected against so-called diploma mills by the accrediting process. The student unrest and dissatisfaction in the 1960s resulted in a great number of defaults in the federally funded Guaranteed Student Loan Program. The United States Office of Education is presently trying to equate educational quality with eligibility for federal funding. Previously, the states had concluded that state approval, registration, or licensure was synonymous with federal approval. The Office of Education has now defined eligibility to be approval by the state, accreditation by the voluntary accrediting agency, and a recognition of eligibility by this federal agency. This would mean that in order for a student to receive educational funds under the Guaranteed Student Loan Program the school of nursing would have to have a state-approved program, be accredited by the National League for Nursing, and be recognized as eligible by the United States Office of Education.

The accountability to students in higher education is becoming a matter of increasing importance. In March 1974, in Denver, Colorado, the Education Commission of the United States called for the first conference on consumer protection in higher education programs. The Commission made several recommendations. It was decided that there should be a means available at each institution and within each state to handle student complaints. The United States Office of Education should continually review the standards being used by recognized accrediting bodies. The Education Commission of the United States should maintain a data bank of information on all higher education programs. This information should be made available to prospective students, students, counselors, parents, and all others affected as consumers of higher education services [9].

A follow-up conference was designated to be held in November 1974, in Knoxville, Tennessee. It was during this second conference in Knoxville that one of the seminar groups dealt with the question of student and institutional rights and responsibilities. The suggested student rights were

Widest access to information on alternatives and post secondary education
Adequate institutional disclosure at all stages: prior to and during entrance, while a student, during and after exit
Clearly presented grievance and redress procedures
No impairment of student-school relations through sale of loans or notes
Provision for maintenance of records [9].

The student responsibilities suggested were

Making educational decisions based upon available information
Meeting financial obligation for services rendered [9].

Those rights accorded to institutions were

Clear knowledge of accreditation, state and federal ground rules
Adequate time to plan for shift in government policies
Clearly presented grievance and redress procedures by accreditation and government agencies
Use of financially responsible refund policies [9].

The responsibilities given to the institutions were [9]

Full Disclosure
Maintenance of student records and provisions for student access to them
Notification to students of financial impact of dropping out
Timely refunds and clear refund policies.*

This is a new type of accountability and it will pervade both the life of the student and the life of the institution. The United States Supreme Court, in the case of *Tinker v. Des Moines*, ruled that

Students in schools as well as out of schools . . . are possessed of fundamental rights which the State must respect, just as they themselves must respect their obligations to the State [10].

Every educational institution in the United States attempts to teach respect for the United States Constitution and the Bill of Rights but, like parents, they actually teach more by actions than by words. The civil rights of students were defined by the Supreme Court in *Tinker v. Des Moines*. The

*Copyright August 1975, The American Journal of Nursing Company. Reproduced with permission from *Nursing Outlook*, Vol. 23, No. 8.

states are now attempting to deal with that decision by passing state legislation that is frequently labeled the *Student's Bill of Rights*. Every faculty member of a school of nursing is affected by this type of legislation. A nursing faculty member should request from her state legislator a copy of the student's bill of rights that applies to her institution. This type of legislation determines to whom a student's grade should be sent, what records can be kept within a student's files, who has access to the student's file, how to appeal a student grievance beyond the scope of the individual institution, and how the school attempts to avoid discrimination in admission requirements. It is evident that the nursing facility should have legal counsel helping them plan for release of information from their students' records to future employers or other institutions of higher learning. The educational institution, the faculty members, and the students need adequate protection in contractual agreements between the school of nursing and the health agencies offering clinical experience to the student nurses.

The federal requirements for student rights are being monitored by the Department of Health, Education, and Welfare. Within 45 days of a request, parents, and students over 18 years old, must be allowed access to student records and are entitled to a clear explanation of the records. Students who find fault with their records, believing them to be wrong, misleading, or irrelevant, may demand a hearing with school officials. Schools must have written permission to make records available to persons outside the school. Students may register complaints with the Department of Health, Education, and Welfare, and if a school fails to uphold the law, federal funds will be discontinued to that institution [11].

Nursing education has a dual accountability, for it must meet the need of the student for a quality education and the need of society for professionals capable of meeting its health needs. We agree with Marlene Kramer who, in her book *Reality Shock*, stated that schools of nursing must help their students to understand the reality of the health care field today and to help make what is now seen as an ideal become a reality. Graduates of schools of nursing must realize that they will have some skills that are not marketable at the time of their graduation. Guided clinical experiences should provide the student nurse with an ability to function in the health care field as it presently exists without losing her vision and capability to function in what it is hoped will be a better future.

Dorothy Mereness suggested six freedoms and responsibilities for student nurses:

(1) Freedom to disagree
(2) Freedom to explore ideas
(3) Freedom to help choose educational goals
(4) Freedom to study independently

(5)   Freedom to experiment
(6)   Freedom to know faculty [12]

These freedoms are based on faith in the student's abilities and eagerness to learn.

A nurse must like herself before she is capable of liking others or having others like her. Nurses need to establish that they are human beings who have rights and needs. In order for nurses to be able to minister to the needs of others, they need to have their own needs fulfilled. Those who minister to the needs of others have long been focusing their lives on responsibility to others, and only recently have women and nurses begun to speak out about their own rights. Every nurse should be allowed to express her feelings. She should be allowed to grow physically and mentally in accord with her innate abilities and have her basic needs of food, clothing, and shelter met. She should also have her spiritual needs met and be fairly compensated for work that she does. In this way, she will be able to obtain satisfaction in her relationships with other human beings. A nurse, who is an advocate for patient rights, must not neglect her own needs or the needs of her co-workers or subordinates. We are firm believers that with every right comes a responsibility. Taking responsibility implies being answerable or accountable for one's work or duty.

WOMEN'S RIGHTS

The nursing profession, being historically made up of women, has played a submissive and dependent role. There are power and leverage for the independent function of nursing in the new nurse practice acts; however, the majority of nurses today are not aware of the leverage nor have they grasped the power. Women did not receive the right to vote in this country until the ratification of the nineteenth amendment in 1920. In the years since then, the lawmakers of this country have challenged discrimination based on the diverse factors of race, creed, and age, but they have not been successful in addressing themselves to discrimination based on the most basic difference—sex.

The National Organization for Women (NOW) is the largest feminist organization in the country at present. As a group, it is working toward passage of the Equal Rights Amendment, declaring that women will only achieve equality by accepting fully their share of the responsibilities. The Equal Rights Amendment was proposed by Congress on March 22, 1972, and is made up of the following three parts:

(1)   Equality of rights under the law shall not be denied or abridged by the United States or by any state on account of sex.
(2)   The Congress shall have the power to enforce, by appropriate legislation, the provisions of this article.

(3)   This amendment shall take effect two years after the date of ratification [13].

State ratification is still needed; as of the fall of 1975, 34 states had ratified the Equal Rights Amendment. The League of Women Voters in their Fall 1975 issue of *Voter* reported on a Roper Research, Inc., poll, completed in June 1975, of a small but representative cross section of adults within the continental United States. The poll showed that 61 percent of those interviewed were in favor of the Equal Rights Amendment. Twenty percent of the sample were opposed and 19 percent had mixed feelings about ERA. The 39 percent who were not in favor of the amendment indicated they felt that men and women were different, that women should have certain courtesies as the gentler sex; or they feared that women having equality might destroy the social institutions of marriage and family and that women would be eligible for the draft. It is interesting that 80 percent of the men interviewed supported the Equal Rights Amendment, as opposed to only 57 percent of the women [13]. To be sure, for women to expect equal rights they must be willing to take equal responsibility.

NURSES' RIGHTS
The Michigan State Nurses' Association's resolution on nurses' rights has become a model in the United States [14].

RESOLVED, That the nurse practitioner has the responsibility to inform employers, present and prospective, of her educational preparation, experience, clinical competencies and those ethical beliefs which would affect her practice, and be it,
RESOLVED, That the nurse practitioner has the responsibility to alter, adjust to or withdraw from situations which are in conflict with her preparation, competencies and beliefs, and be it,
RESOLVED, That the employer shall provide the resources through which health services are made available to the recipient, and be it,
RESOLVED, That the nurse practitioner has the right and responsibility to collaborate with her/his employer to create an environment which promotes and assures the delivery of optimal health services, and be it further,
RESOLVED, That the nurse has a right to expect that her/his employer will respect her/his competencies, values and individual differences as they relate to her/his practice.*

It is evident that nurses' rights and responsibilities are closely related. But we contend nurses are quite committed to their responsibilities and only recently have begun to become concerned about their rights. Do nurses feel it takes away from their professionalism to be concerned about the compensation they receive for their work? Status in the United States has historically been based on economic rewards. Nurses need to toot their own horns, polish their own images, and lobby for support from the society that they have long served. The right to self-expression, the right to control one's practice and environment, the right to control one's profession and set standards for nursing, are all of importance to the nurse. When the public sees nursing as separate from and interdependent with the medical profession, nursing will no longer have to struggle to achieve professional rights. The present dissatisfaction of the public with both medical and hospital services can be taken advantage of by the nursing profession if nurses validate their concern for health care consumers by giving constructive answers to their complaints.

Using the 1970 census and the health resources statistics, Bullough and Bullough gave evidence of how greatly sex discrimination pervades the health profession. The median income in dollars of those professions dominated by men far outranks the income of those dominated by women. Even in the nursing profession, where 94 percent of all registered nurses are women, the male nurse's median income was $7,013, while that of the female nurse was $5,603 [15].

Accountability has been referred to as the payment of dues for the increased economic status and independence being enjoyed by nurses today. There is power in this independence. The nursing profession must be willing to be both legally and ethically responsible for the care it gives. In the past nursing has been held accountable, but not to the consumer of its health care. Rather, it has been held accountable to the medical profession or to the institution or agency by which its members were employed. However, the hallmark of professionalism is the ability to monitor what is acceptable performance for the profession within the profession itself. The patient comes into the hospital trusting that the nurses and doctors will give him the best possible care that their professions can offer. In response to this trust, the American Nurses' Association developed a code of ethics that indicates the profession's acceptance of this responsibility. The *Code for Nurses* describes ten areas of accountability as follows:

(1) The nurse provides services with respect for human dignity and the uniqueness of the client unrestricted by considerations of social or economic status, personal attributes, or the nature of health problems.

(2) The nurse safeguards the client's right to privacy by judiciously protecting information of a confidential nature.

(3) The nurse acts to safeguard the client and the public when health care and safety are affected by the incompetent, unethical, or illegal practice of any person.

(4) The nurse assumes responsibility and accountability for individual nursing judgments and actions.

(5) The nurse maintains competence in nursing.

(6) The nurse exercises informed judgment and uses individual compe-

     tence and qualifications as criteria in seeking consultation, accepting responsibilities, and delegating nursing activities to others.

(7) The nurse participates in activities that contribute to the ongoing development of the profession's body of knowledge.

(8) The nurse participates in the profession's efforts to implement and improve standards of nursing.

(9) The nurse participates in the profession's efforts to establish and maintain conditions of employment conducive to high quality nursing care.

(10) The nurse participates in the profession's effort to protect the public from misinformation and misrepresentation and to maintain the integrity of nursing.

(11) The nurse collaborates with members of the health professions and other citizens in promoting community and national efforts to meet the health needs of the public.

The profession of nursing further demonstrated that it had accepted this accountability when the American Nurses' Association placed as its first priority for the 1974-1975 biennium the improvement of the practice of nursing by implementation of standards for the practice of nursing developed by the Congress for Nursing Practice. The American Nurses' Association is a professional association that has organized nurses to band together and achieve as a group what they would be incapable of achieving as individuals. Members of a professional organization should not meet together merely because they share a common occupation, but rather to ensure the competent performance of their professional functions. Professional organizations meet to develop and ensure the highest attainable standards for the profession, to educate the public as to what their expectation should be of the profession, and to provide for the protection of the public against those professionals who blatantly disregard professional standards. This concern for the quality of service rendered to the public is essential for the protection of both the public and the nursing profession itself. The American Nurses' Association believes that "A profession that does not maintain the confidence of the public will soon cease to be a social force" [17]. The new standards focus on nursing practice and are a means of fulfilling the profession's obligation to provide improved nursing practice. They acknowledge nursing's primary responsibility and accountability for the care given to its clients. The standards are based on a systematic approach to nursing practice which is generally spoken of as nursing process. Nursing process is a thought process and not a series of distinct, overt steps. The process can be described simply as assessment, planning, implementation, and evaluation. The Congress for Nursing Practice established *Standards for Nursing Practice*, which apply to nursing practice in any setting.

    Standard 1. The collection of data about the health status of the client/patient is systematic and continuous. The data are accessible, communicative, and recorded.

Standard 2. Nursing diagnoses are derived from health status data.

Standard 3. The plan of nursing care includes goals derived from the nursing diagnoses.

Standard 4. The plan of nursing care includes priorities and the prescribed nursing approaches or measures to achieve the goals derived from the nursing diagnoses.

Standard 5. Nursing actions provide for client/patient participation in health promotion, maintenance and restoration.

Standard 6. Nursing actions assist the client/patient to maximize his health capabilities.

Standard 7. The client's/patient's progress or lack of progress toward goal achievement is determined by the client/patient and the nurse.

Standard 8. The client's/patient's progress or lack of progress toward goal acheivement directs reassessment, reordering of priorities, new goal setting and a revision of the plan of nursing care [17].

In addition to these standards for nursing practice applicable to all settings, the Congress for Nursing Practice developed separate standards for community health, geriatric, maternal-child health, mental health, and medical-surgical nursing practices. Each of these sets of standards is available in booklet form from the American Nurses' Association.

Are nurses presently fulfilling the *Standards of Nursing Practice?* The recent use of nursing audits to evaluate patient care received has shown that if nurses are fulfilling these standards of nursing practice, there is no documented evidence in nursing records. With the current nurse-patient ratios, is it possible to achieve these standards of nursing care, or are these standards only ideal goals impossible to attain? This is an important question to answer, for if the American Nurses' Association maintains that these are the standards of nursing practice for the profession, failure to meet these standards could result in legal action against nurses. These professional standards definitely need to be related to the other policies and procedures that govern the nurse's practice within an institution or agency. The gap needs to be closed between the actual practice of nurses within the profession and what are defined as nursing functions within the new nurse practice acts. If the institution, and *not* the nursing profession, controls the nurse-patient ratio, how can a nurse then be held accountable for the quality of nursing care given?

We believe that nursing is fortunate to have the National League for Nursing, its accrediting body for both nursing education and nursing service, separate from its professional organization. Both the lay public and the nursing profession are represented in the membership of the National League for Nursing. This is a true strength, allowing for consumer representation in the nursing profession. At a time when consumerism is having such a great effect on the health profession, nursing is fortunate to have a history of consumer interest. It is also fortunate to have nonprofessionals in the National League for Nursing from whom the consumer point of view can be elicited. Such nonprofessional membership in this organization enhances broad-based support for nursing.

PROFESSIONAL REVIEW AND QUALITY CONTROL

The decisions made daily by the professional nurse may be based on scientific absolutes or may have a basis in ethical considerations. To achieve the standards of care adopted by the American Nurses' Association, the nurse must be able to use both empirical evidence and knowledge of the non-scientific disciplines in order to meet her patient's needs. Nursing is therefore considered to be not only a science, but also an art. The nursing process is a mental process based on both logical evaluation of information and intuitive interpretation.

Is there a *quality* of nursing practice? Nursing has not met the qualification of professionalism by developing an ethical code and standards of practice; it must be accountable for nursing practice. How will the profession monitor its own performance? The United States Congress recently passed legislation calling for Professional Standards Review Organizations (PSRO) as one means to help regulate both the cost and the quality of health care. Consumer groups appear to be questioning whether health professionals can be counted on to regulate the quality and cost of care to the best interest of the public. The professionals are questioning whether consumer representation on such boards would mean consumer control of professional judgments. In nursing, peer review has been defined as

The evaluation by practicing professional nurses of the quality of nursing care performed by other nurses according to stated norms of the profession [18].

In this context, peer review could be of an individual nurse or of the nursing care given within an institution or agency. A peer group for health care could be made up of physicians, nurses, physical therapists, medical social workers, and nutritionists. Most nurses are employed within bureaucracies and are subjected to a great deal of authoritarian control. It is widely accepted that professionals are able to judge quite accurately the quality of a peer's work. The trick is to get them to tell what they know. It is true that there is a great deal of self-protection within professional groups, at great expense to the public they serve.

If the nursing profession fails to control the quality of nursing practice, governmental regulations will become more stringent. In attempting to provide for quality control of health care, much can be learned from industrial standards. Any quality control program has three components: standards, surveillance, and corrective action. Accrediting agencies for nursing care have in the past evaluated health care institutions for structures that would permit quality nursing care. In other words, they determined whether conditions existed under which good nursing care was likely to take place, but did not determine whether quality nursing care actually resulted. One means of providing quality control in nursing service is to have a PSRO perform a nursing audit. In order to perform the audit, the agency must first define the nursing practice criteria. A system must then be devised to compare the actual nursing practice with the criteria for nursing practice. An acceptable level of practice must then be decided on. Anyone can determine whether the structure exists in which quality care can take place, but it requires professional judgment to determine whether such care is actually being delivered. Quality control forms to be used in nursing audits could be individualized to cover the nursing functions of a particular patient unit, or they could be devised as a form applicable to all patients with a specific disease entity. The nursing care audits known to us have been completed by community health agencies in eastern Pennsylvania. These audits have almost unanimously proved the nursing profession's inability to communicate by providing adequate documentation of the nursing care given. How can nurses prove what they don't document? The criteria have been set, the surveillance has been completed, and corrective action now needs to be taken to ensure accurate documentation of nursing care given. The Joint Commission on Accreditation of Hospitals further requires of nursing audits that a follow-up study be carried out to determine if the corrective action is effective. A report of the audit is to be made to the body to which the nurse is accountable [19]. A nursing audit appears to be an excellent method of providing for quality control of nursing care, especially if the peer review is shared by community professionals outside the institution or agency being evaluated.

Funding agencies, whether private insurance companies or government agencies at the state or federal level, have forced the nursing profession to examine its quality control systems by carefully scrutinizing records and care prior to the receipt of funds. With the record review becoming a prime means of quality control of the nursing profession, legally acceptable limits have to be set to prevent invasion of the rights of privacy of the patient. In an effort to meet the requirements of the PSRO and to complete nursing audits, the information in the patient's chart is reviewed by a host of nurses, physicians, supporting health professionals, accountants, and statisticians. Many of these people are not even closely connected with the patient or the health agency. The abuse of such wide dissemination of patient information is of grave concern to nurses who ethically support the right to privacy of the patient.

Every nurse must acknowledge the need for improvement in the quality of nursing care. Nursing must proclaim its flaws and assume responsibility for correcting its problems. The individual nurse assumes such responsibility in belonging to a professional organization, in volunteering for the time-consuming activity of nursing audits, and by spending time explaining the nursing profession's goals to the lay public. A good quality-control system will provide the data necessary for non-nurse administrators to visualize the the price they are paying in quality of care when they decrease the number of professional nursing personnel in order to meet economic limitations. Nurse participation in peer review and in quality control of health care is needed to balance increasing regulatory decision-making by the federal and state governments. There is no way nursing can "beat" the consumers of health care services. So how about joining them to make quality nursing care become a reality!

REFERENCES

1. Farber, Doris. *Enough! The revolt of the american consumer.* New York: Farrar, Straus and Giroux, 1972. P. 28.
2. *Ibid.*, p. 62.
3. *Ibid.*, p. 108.
4. *Ibid.*, p. 110.
5. American Hospital Association. *Patient's Bill of Rights.* Chicago, Illinois, 1972.
6. Minnesota Laws of 1973, Chapter 688.
7. Southwestern Michigan Inservice Education Council. *The dying person's bill of rights.* Lansing, Michigan, 1974.
8. O'Connor v. Donaldson. 95 Supreme Court 2486, 1975.
9. Millard, Richard M. The new accountability. *Nurs. Outlook* 23:496, 1975.
10. Schimmel, David, and Fisher, Louis. *The civil rights of students.* New York: Harper & Row, 1975.
11. Wells, Chris. News to use. *Family Circle* 87:48, 1975.
12. Pearson, Betty D. Issues of student clinical nursing. *J. Nurs. Ed.* 14:20, 1975.
13. ERA: What we have in common. *Voter* 25:5, 1975.
14. Fagin, Claire M. Nurses' rights. *Am. J. Nurs.* 75:82, 1975.
15. Bullough, Bonnie, and Bullough, Vern L. Sex discrimination in health care. *Nurs. Outlook* 23:42, 1975.
16. American Nurses' Association. *Code for nurses with interpretive statements.* Kansas City, Missouri, 1976.
17. American Nurses' Association. Standards of nursing practice. *Am. Nurse* 6:11, 1974.
18. Ramphal, Marjories. Peer review. *Am. J. Nurs.* 74:64, 1974.
19. JCAH standard for nursing audits. *Nursing'75* 5:72, 1975.

9. COLLECTIVE BARGAINING AND THE NURSE EMPLOYMENT CONTRACT

In the past twenty years, American nurses have seen their role constantly evolving into one of more truly professional status. With the increasing emphasis on professional education for nurses at the collegiate and post-graduate level, the self-image, aspirations, and goals of the profession have been changing as well. Nurses are no longer willing to fulfill a sub-servient role in the health care field and to have their economic progress based on the altruistic impulses or the guilt feelings of their employers. We live in a highly competitive society in which each group must aggressively compete for its piece of the economic pie or fall hopelessly behind in the race. Nurses have had before them the examples of similar groups, such as teachers, who, although devoted to the welfare of society, were objects of pity and scorn because of their low economic status. Through collective bargaining procedures and aggressive pursuit of their economic goals, teachers quickly assumed an economic status more in accord with their educational attainments and responsibilities. The nursing profession, although somewhat more reluctant to assert itself, soon followed suit.

Although nonprofit health care institutions, the usual employers of nurses, were originally excluded from the provisions of the Taft-Hartley Act, which set the guidelines for most collective bargaining in the United States, nurse lobbyists continually importuned state legislators for laws providing for collective bargaining in such nonprofit institutions. As a result, many states enacted such laws prior to 1974. The first great federal labor legislation enacted during the days of the New Deal was the Wagner Act of 1935, out of which evolved the Taft-Hartley Act of 1947. Due to the influence of various hospital associations, nonprofit health care institutions were excluded from the protection of the National Labor Relations Board under the terms of the Taft-Hartley Act as it was originally enacted in 1947 [1]. Of course, this was very detrimental to nurses seeking to raise their economic status and attain professional recognition. The enactment of laws providing for mandatory collective bargaining by nonprofit health care institutions by approximately 12 states was a help [2], but nevertheless nurses did not achieve full legal equality in the area of labor relations until the 1974 amendment to the Taft-Hartley Act, which brought nonprofit health care institutions under the jurisdiction of the National Labor Relations Board [3].

THE SUPERVISOR AS A MEMBER
OF THE BARGAINING UNIT

A constantly recurring problem in the area of labor relations for nurses is the role of the supervisor. According to section 2(11) of the National Labor Relations Act

The term *supervisor* means any individual having authority, in the interest of the employer, to hire, transfer, suspend, lay-off, recall, promote, discharge, assign, reward or discipline other employees, or responsibility to direct them, or to adjust their grievances, or effectively to recommend such action, if in connection with the foregoing the exercise of such authority is not of a merely routine or clerical nature, but requires the use of independent judgment.

Under the terms of the National Labor Relations Act, supervisors are part of management and are therefore prohibited from participating in what are referred to as protected activities under the terms of the National Labor Relations Act. These protected activities are of an infinite variety but generally relate to efforts by employees to organize, obtain recognition from an employer, and bargain collectively. Supervisors are prohibited from participating in such activities, even though they may be promoting the interests of the employees.

The question that usually presents itself is whether an individual commonly referred to as a nurse supervisor is actually a supervisor within the meaning of the National Labor Relations Act. There is a considerable body of opinion that holds that such individuals are not truly supervisors in the sense of the National Labor Relations Act, since their authority is not of a truly managerial variety and the supervision which they exercise is more of a professional nature, involving the supervision of health care delivery. Such a distinction must, of course, be made and decisions are made on a case-by-case basis depending on the authority given a particular individual in a particular institution.

There are many arguments in favor of including supervisors and head nurses, whose positions are certainly analogous, within the bargaining unit since they offer the other employees leadership that they might not otherwise have. The argument against such inclusion is that supervisors and head nurses have a dual loyalty and the bargaining unit may find out to its detriment that the primary loyalty of such individuals is to management. Nevertheless, even if such supervisors and head nurses are supervisors within the meaning of the National Labor Relations Act, they are not thereby prohibited from joining state nursing associations, which act as the representatives of bargaining units in labor negotiations under the Taft-Hartley Act. The only requirement is that such supervisors be insulated from the actual bargaining process and from protected activities of the bargaining units [4].

The progress the nursing profession has made as a result of favorable labor legislation and an awakening of interest in collective bargaining must be conceived as a two-pronged thrust. The first and, in the view of most nurses and ourselves, the most important thrust is toward improved working conditions. Working conditions include both salaries and such items as nurse-patient ratio, safety precautions, and hours of employment. Certainly without adequate compensations, it is difficult for a nurse to think of herself as a professional. Nursing has lagged behind other fields with comparable educational requirements for too long, but is now rapidly gaining the lost ground. Although it cannot be said that these gains have come easily or without resistance from many hospitals and other health care providers employing nurses, the progress has certainly been dramatic.

As regards the other thrust of collective bargaining, which is for shared governance, or a voice in management, progress has been much slower. It has been fairly typical of professional groups to wish for a voice in management. Teachers' associations have been clamoring for such representation for years and nurses are now asserting themselves as well. Leaders in the nursing profession believe that nurses have a right to insist on a share in decisions involving patient care and quality assurance. They have suggested as one goal of collective bargaining the incorporation of a policy development group in the form of a nursing practice council with equal representation from the nursing service administration and the staff nurses of the collective bargaining unit [5].

Predictably, management has resisted these demands for shared governance with a great deal of vigor and tenacity. The feeling is prevalent among many directors, both in the health care field and in other fields as well, that to accede to the demand that they abdicate management prerogatives in the face of what they conceive to be insatiable demands for increased economic benefits would be to invite anarchy. In any event, progress in the field of shared governance has been much slower than in the area of working conditions [6]. To be sure, a change in working conditions can result in improved health care, the obvious example being in the field of nurse-patient ratios and staffing [7].

THE NATIONAL LABOR RELATIONS ACT

It might be well at this point to take a closer look at the National Labor Relations Act, the provisions of which apply to most collective bargaining activities in which nurses are currently engaged. By the very nature of their profession, nurses most often find themselves in the role of employee rather than employer and therefore have a vital interest in the rights of employees as protected by section 7 of the National Labor Relations Act. There is a vast body of law interpreting the provisions of section 7 and, of necessity, we shall only discuss them in a relatively superficial manner in this text.

Examples of protected activities covered by section 7 of the National Labor Relations Act that apply directly to the nursing profession are the following:

Forming or attempting to form a union among the employees of a company.
Joining a union whether the union is recognized by the employer or not.
Assisting a union to organize the employees of an employer.
Going out on strike to secure better working conditions.
Refraining from activity in behalf of a union [8].

One of the rights protected by section 7 is the right of employees to enter into a union security agreement with their employer. This agreement is frequently referred to by the public as a union shop or a closed shop. Nurses who have organized and are represented by a collective bargaining unit have a right to enter an agreement with their hospital whereby all members of the bargaining unit must be union members, and new nurses that are hired have a thirty-day grace period in which to join the union. It is very possible that such union shop contracts will become more common as nurses become more cognizant of the necessity to pursue aggressively their economic goals in order to maintain their professional status in our society.

Another right that is basic to all collective bargaining is the ultimate weapon of an employee, the right to strike. Striking is, in effect, economic warfare and is as abhorrent to most employees as warfare is to most citizens in general. However, as in the case of relations between nations, without the ability and willingness to use force under certain circumstances, there can be no true bargaining. Under the provisions of sections 7 and 8 of the National Labor Relations Act, employees are guaranteed the right to strike, with certain limitations and qualifications. In general, it may be said that the National Labor Relations Act protects strikers engaged in lawful strikes by giving them a right to reinstatement in their jobs.

Strikes

Strikes under the terms of the National Labor Relations Act are of two kinds: the economic strike and the unfair labor practice strike. An economic strike is one in which strikers seek economic benefits, such as higher wages, better working conditions, and shorter hours. Such strikers are called economic strikers. While they cannot be discharged for going on strike, they can be replaced. For example, a nurse who goes on strike for higher wages can be replaced by the hospital by a bona fide permanent replacement. If the replacement nurse is filling the striking nurse's position at the time the striker agrees unconditionally to return to work, the hospital is not required to reinstate the striking nurse at that time. However, if such a striking nurse does not obtain regular and substantially equivalent employment, she will be entitled to be recalled and given first preference on jobs for which she is qualified at the hospital when vacancies occur [9].

If a group of nurses go on strike to protest an unfair labor practice by a hospital employer, such strikers can be neither discharged nor permanently replaced. If the striking nurses do not commit serious misconduct while on strike, they are entitled to resume their jobs after the strike ends, even if a substitute or replacement hired to do their work must be discharged. If the hospital fails to rehire them at the end of the strike and they have made an unconditional request for reinstatement and been unlawfully denied that reinstatement by the hospital, then, on recourse to the National Labor Relations Board, they may be awarded back pay from the time they should have been reinstated.

Of course, employees who engage in unlawful strikes are not entitled to these reinstatement privileges. Strikes are considered unlawful if their objectives are unlawful. For instance, a strike in support of an unfair labor practice by a union would be unlawful, just as would a strike to compel an employer to commit an unfair labor practice. Strikes in violation of a "no strike provision" of a collective bargaining contract are unlawful. It has been held by the United States Supreme Court that sit-down strikes are unlawful. These are strikes where employees not only refuse to work, but occupy the employer's property, thereby depriving him of the use of it [10]. Such strikes have not been common in the health care industry but could conceivably occur in the future.

In addition to loss of reinstatement privileges by engaging in an unlawful strike, nurses and other employees could lose their reinstatement privileges under the National Labor Relations Act because of serious misconduct in the course of a strike that would otherwise be lawful. Examples of conduct that could be considered serious misconduct of a nature to deprive strikers of the right to reinstatement would be

1. Strikers threatening violence against nonstriking employees entering a hospital;

2. Strikers physically blocking nurses and other personnel from entering or leaving a struck hospital; and

3. Strikers attacking management representatives.

While misconduct of this nature is rare in the health care field, it must not be eliminated as a possibility in the future, since we have all seen the violence that sometimes attends teachers' strikes in which the striking employees have educational attainments comparable to those of nurses [11].

One of the most important provisions of the National Labor Relations Act concerns certain "mandatory" matters in regard to which neither the employers nor the employees may refuse to bargain collectively. These mandatory matters include wages, hours, and other terms or conditions of employment, the negotiation of an agreement, and any question arising under an agreement. While the National Labor Relations Act does not require one party to agree to a proposal by the other, it is unfair labor practice for either party to refuse to bargain collectively with the other in regard to mandatory subjects.

Under the provisions of section 8(d) of the National Labor Relations Act, neither party to a collective bargaining agreement that is actually in effect may unilaterally change the provisions of the contract unless it takes the following steps:

1. The party wishing to make the change must notify the other party to the contract in writing at least 60 days before the date on which the collective bargaining agreement is to expire;

2. The party wishing to make the change must offer to meet and confer with the other party in an attempt to reach an agreement about the proposed change;

3. The party wishing to make the change must, within 30 days after the written notice of the intended change to the other party, notify the Federal Mediation and Conciliation Service of the existence of dispute if in fact one exists; and

4. The party desiring the change must continue to adhere to all the terms of the existing contract for at least 60 days after the written notice to the other party, or until the date the existing contract expires, whichever is later, before resorting to a strike or a lockout.

The reader may well ask if it is not inconsistent to say that neither party is required to make a concession to the other on so-called mandatory matters, while neither may refuse to bargain in good faith. An examination of the meaning of "bargaining in good faith" under the terms of the National Labor Relations Act will show that there is no actual inconsistency. In order to be bargaining in good faith the employer must agree to meet at reasonable times with whomever is designated as the employees' representative to carry on the negotiations. The employer may not object to or dictate the selection of the employees' representative. The employer is also required in good faith bargaining to supply to the employees' representative whatever information is relevant and necessary to allow such a representative to bargain intelligently and effectively with respect to conditions of employment, such as wages and hours. The foregoing does not imply, however, an obligation on the part of either party to reach an agreement.

The following are examples of violations of section 8(a)(5) of the National Labor Relations Act which require good faith bargaining on mandatory subjects:

1. Refusal by the representative of the hospital administration to meet with the representative of the nurses' bargaining unit because the nurses are out on strike;

2. Insistence by hospital management, prior to a breakdown of negotiations, on a contract provision that all nurses will be polled by secret ballot before their bargaining unit calls a strike;

3. Refusal by hospital management to supply a representative of the nurses' bargaining unit with cost and other data concerning a group insurance plan covering such nurses; and

4. An announcement by hospital management of a wage increase without consulting the representative of the nurses' bargaining unit.

Under section 8(b)(1)(A) of the National Labor Relations Act, it is an unfair labor practice for a labor organization to "restrain or coerce employees in the exercise of rights guaranteed in section 7," which rights are generally referred to as protected activities. While a union may use reasonable means to enforce organizational discipline, certain acts are prohibited and constitute unlawful coercion under the provision of the National Labor Relations Act.

Examples of actions by a union that would constitute unlawful coercion and therefore an unfair labor practice under section 8(b)(1)(A) of the Act include, but are not limited to, the following:

1. Mass picketing by such numbers of striking health service employees that nonstriking employees are physically barred from entering a hospital;

2. Acts of force or violence on the picket line by striking hospital service employees;

3. Threats by striking nurses to do bodily injury to nonstriking nurses;

4. Threatening nurses that they will lose their positions unless they support the activities of the union; and

5. A statement made to a nurse who opposes representation by a union that she will lose her job if the union wins the majority in her hospital or health agency.

In cases in which a union is the exclusive bargaining representative for a group of nurses, it would be an unfair labor practice for a union to refuse to process a grievance in retaliation for the nurses' criticism of union officers. It would also be an unfair labor practice for a union representing a group of nurses to reject an application for referral to a job in a unit represented by a union based on the applicant's race or union activities.

The National Labor Relations Act makes it an unfair labor practice to *featherbed*, or to use coercion to force an employer to hire and pay for an employee who serves no useful purpose. As set forth in section 8(b)(6) of the Act, it is an unfair labor practice "to cause or attempt to cause an employer to pay or deliver or agree to pay or deliver any money or thing of value, in the nature of an exaction, for services which are not performed or not to be performed." Although understaffing rather than overstaffing is the general rule in the field of nursing, it is conceivable that as the position of nursing bargaining units becomes stronger as a result of collective bargaining, attempts may be made to featherbed. This will be an even greater possibility if present trends continue and the supply of nurses exceeds the demand.

The National Labor Relations Board

At all times since its initial enactment in 1935, the National Labor Relations Act has been administered by the National Labor Relations Board. The National Labor Relations Board, consisting of a general council and staff and five members, each with his own staff, has two primary functions. The first is to conduct secret ballot elections to determine whether a majority of employees in a unit appropriate for collective bargaining desire a given union to represent them in their collective bargaining procedures. The second function is to prevent and rectify unfair labor practices that are committed by employers or unions.

In order to initiate action by the National Labor Relations Board in the field of a representation election or rectification of an unfair labor practice, it is necessary for the party desiring relief to complete and file a printed form known as a petition, in the case of matters relating to elections, and a charge in the case of matters relating to unfair labor practices. These forms may be obtained at and filed with a regional office of the National Labor Relations Board in the area where the unit of employees is located. The petition and the charge must both be completed under oath.

In the case of a petition for an election, section 9(c)(1) of the Act provides that

The Board shall investigate such petition and if it has reasonable cause to believe that a question of representation affecting commerce exists, shall provide for an appropriate hearing upon due notice.

If, after such a hearing is held, the Board finds that such a question exists, it shall then direct that a secret ballot representation election be held "and shall certify the results thereof." When more than three groups are on the ballot, a runoff election shall be held for the two receiving the highest number of votes. If, after this election, a union receives a majority of the votes cast, it is certified as the collective bargaining representative for the unit and it is an unfair labor practice for an employer to refuse to bargain with a union thus certified.

In the case of a charge filed with the National Labor Relations Board alleging an unfair labor practice, the Board will initially conduct an investigation. If, as a result of this investigation, the Board has reason to believe that an unfair labor practice has been committed, it will issue a complaint which will be served on the party accused of committing such unfair labor practice. A hearing will be held before a National Labor Relations Board trial examiner who will make findings and recommendations to the National Labor Relations Board. All parties at the hearing may appeal to the Board from the decision of the trial examiner. Once the Board considers the record and the appeal, if any, it is authorized to issue a cease and desist order against a person or union found to have committed an unfair labor practice.

Under the provisions of the Act, a charge must be filed and served on the offending party within six months after an unfair labor practice is committed.

In a case in which a regional director determines, as a result of the initial investigation, that the facts do not warrant issuing a complaint, an aggrieved party may appeal directly to the general council which has the authority to reverse the regional director. The decisions of the general council in this area are final.

If a party fails to comply with an order of the National Labor Relations Board, the Board may petition the Federal Circuit Court of Appeals for an injunction enforcing such order. A party who defies an injunction issued by the Federal Circuit Court of Appeals may be subject to fine or imprisonment for contempt of court.

Public Law 93-360, effective August 25, 1974, brought one and a half million employees of nonprofit health care institutions within the jurisdiction of the National Labor Relations Board. Due to the vital national interest in preventing unnecessary interruption of health care activity, special provisions were provided for mediation and fact-finding in the case of health care institutions; in addition, there is a requirement for ten days' advance notice before picketing or instituting a strike [12].

The procedures regarding a representation election are identical to those previously provided in the Act and the petitioner for such an election must show that of the workers involved, at least 30 percent have signed union authorization cards or petitions, or by other means have indicated their support of a particular collective bargaining representative.

As with other industries and groups, only one representation election may be held within any 12-month period in a particular employee unit.

All the provisions defining unfair labor practices in the Act prior to the 1974 amendment also apply today to the health care industry. However, in an attempt to minimize the possibility of interruptions in the delivery of health care, section 8(g) was incorporated into the Act by the 1974 amendment. Under the provisions of this section, a labor organization is prohibited from striking or picketing a health care facility without first giving ten days' advance notice to the employer and to the Federal Mediation and Conciliation Service. According to section 8(g), "Notice shall state the date and time that such action will commence. The notice, once given, may be extended by written agreement of both parties." The 1974 amendment to the National Labor Relations Act provided that, in the case of health care institutions, ninety days' written notice must be served by the employer or union of the intent to terminate or modify a collective bargaining contract. This exceeds by thirty days the sixty-day notice requirement in the case of other industries subject to the jurisdiction of the National Labor Relations Board.

In the case of a health care industry dispute that continues for sixty days, notice must be given to the Federal Mediation and Conciliation Service and similar state agencies under the provision of the 1974 amendment.

In the case of a dispute in the health care area involving an initial contract, thirty days' notice must be given by the union to the employer, the Federal Mediation and Conciliation Service, and the appropriate state agency before a strike can be called.

Whether a dispute involves contract termination, modification, or a negotiation of an initial contract, the Federal Mediation and Conciliation Service has the right to issue a thirty-day no strike, no lock-out order and set up a fact-finding board to take evidence and make settlement recommendations in connection with continuing attempts at mediation and conciliation. When all the provisions of the 1974 amendment to the Act have failed to prevent a strike, at the very last instance, a ten-day strike or picketing notice must be given.

It is apparent that Congress, in its decision to bring nonprofit health care institutions within the jurisdiction of the National Labor Relations Board, was well aware of the devastating effects that strikes and other job actions might have on health care delivery and the vital interest of the public in uninterrupted health care delivery. The 1974 amendment broadens the authority of the National Labor Relations Board in the area of health care to allow it to delay strikes and attempt conciliation and mediation. The provisions of the Act, in regard to preventing interruptions in health care delivery, stop short of imposing *binding arbitration*, or forcing the parties to a labor dispute to abide by the decision of an arbitrator.

While consumer groups might argue that it was against the public interest to extend the jurisdiction of the National Labor Relations Board to one and a half million employees who had not previously been covered, it must be pointed out that these employees are citizens too and to deprive them of the protection of the National Labor Relations Board and the right to strike would be tantamount to giving them second-class citizenship.

Precedents

In conclusion, a word should be said about precedents. Practices not part of a negotiated contract may become part of it. For instance, under certain circumstances, an employer who does not enforce a provision of the contract against one employee who violates it cannot later enforce it against another employee. In other words, the contract has been modified by setting a precedent.

THE NURSE'S EMPLOYMENT CONTRACT

Employment contracts can be made by individual nurses or by groups of nurses. Group contracts for nurses have been the result of administrative decisions in the past, but are likely in the future to be the result of collective bargaining. The individual employment contract provides the nurse with an opportunity to have an employer understand the considerations within the employment situation that the nurse values. What are the nurse's priorities?

It is necessary for the reader to understand the basic principles of contract law in order to fully understand the nurse's employment contract. In its simplest form, it may be said that a contract is a legally enforceable promise. In most cases, an employment contract consists of legally enforceable mutual promises. For example, an employment contract may consist of a promise by an employee to perform specified services at specified times in return for a promise by the employer to give a certain monetary payment and other benefits.

The basic principles of contract law constitute a full year of study at most law schools and, in fact, the subject of contracts constitutes one of the most important and difficult subjects with which a law student must cope. We will touch briefly on some of the basic principles of contract law. Except as otherwise provided by statute, a contract, in order to be legally enforceable, must meet the following criteria:

1. It must result from a "meeting of the minds," or agreement between the contracting parties. That is to say, one party must offer to do something in return for certain stated acts by the other, and the party to whom the offer is made must accept in exactly the same terms. If the acceptance is in different terms, then the acceptance does not constitute a contract but merely a counteroffer. For example, if a nurse offers to work an 8-hour shift as a general duty floor nurse for $40 and the hospital says it

will hire her for $35 per shift, there is no legally enforceable contract but merely a counteroffer by the hospital which must be accepted or rejected by the nurse.

2. In order to be legally enforceable, a promise must be based on consideration, or something of value that is given for the promise. Generally, in nurse employment contracts, the "something of value" that is given for the nurse's promise to perform her professional duties is a reciprocal promise by the hospital to pay an agreed sum.

3. Contracts of employment, if proved, are equally enforceable whether written or oral. It is obvious that it is easier to prove the terms of a written contract than a verbal one.

4. A mere offer to work for a certain amount of money does not constitute a binding contract unless it is accepted. For example, if a nurse offers her services to the hospital personnel department at a given rate of pay, until someone agrees verbally that she should begin work or until she enters a written contract, she is not obligated to perform those services.

5. A contract may be either express or implied; that is, it is not always necessary for the parties to declare the exact terms of the contract in order for it to be binding. For instance, when a hospital puts a nurse to work without discussing her exact rate of pay, the law will imply an agreement by the hospital to pay her a reasonable amount for the work she performs. What is reasonable would be judged by the prevailing rates for similar work in that community. While, as we have previously stated, the terms of the contract are determined by the intent of the parties in the form of an offer and acceptance in identical terms, this intent may be implied from the actions of the parties and the circumstances surrounding their actions. For example, an offer that does not specify a time for acceptance must be accepted within a reasonable time. A nurse who offers to perform services for $10 an hour is not bound by an acceptance five years later when the prevailing rate may be much higher. The law would imply under the circumstances that one term of the offer was that it be accepted within a reasonable time.

6. Under certain circumstances provided by statute, a promise need not be supported by consideration. These circumstances do not generally relate to nurses' contracts but, as a matter of interest, we will mention them briefly. Most states have adopted what is known as the Uniform Written Obligations Act, which provides that a written promise containing a statement that the promisor intends to be legally bound is enforceable even though there is no consideration. Also, under the laws of most states the presence of a seal on a written promise eliminates the need to prove consideration to make the promise enforceable.

To recapitulate, a contract exists by virtue of an offer and an acceptance in identical terms. The offer and acceptance constitute mutual promises and one acts as consideration for the other. Of course, the acceptance must be communicated to the individual making the offer and an offer can be withdrawn at any time before it is accepted. A promise may be legally enforceable without consideration, as in the case of a unilateral promise, if the person to whom the promise is made acts in reliance on the promise to his detriment. Such would be the case if a nurse indicated to a patient that she would report for work the next day and in reliance on her promise, the patient failed to hire someone else, even though the patient had not communicated an acceptance of the nurse's offer of professional services.

The nurse as an employee entering a contract is expected to possess the skills and knowledge needed to perform the services for which she is contracting. The nurse also undertakes to adhere to reasonable rules of conduct and must not carry out her duties in a manner which would cause injury to her employer.

The employer is bound to provide a safe place to work and suitable and safe equipment. An employer of nurses needs to understand the scope of nursing practice and to require only those duties which a nurse is legally allowed to perform. The employer needs to look at and accept a nurse's education and experience as defining the areas of expertise within the nursing profession. Nursing is fast becoming a profession of specialists as technology advances knowledge at a rapid pace. A nurse today may not feel qualified to function in every area of the field of nursing practice. The American Nurses' Association has proposed *Guidelines for the Individual Nurse Contract* (see Appendix I).

REFERENCES
 1. Schutt, Barbara G. Collective action for professional security. *Am. J. Nurs.* 73:1947, 1973.
 2. Lewis, Howard L. Wave of union organizing will follow break in Taft-Hartley dam. *Nurs. Dig.* 3:60, 1975.
 3. Labor Management Relation Act, 1947, as Amended by Public Laws 86-257, 1959, and 93-360, 1974.
 4. Zimmerman, Anne. Models for a multi-purpose organization: The industrial model. *Am. Nurse* 6:7, 1974.
 5. Cleland, Virginia S. A professional model for collective bargaining. *Am. Nurse* 6:11, 1974.
 6. Jacox, Ada K. Who defines and controls nursing practice? *Am. J. Nurs.* 69:978, 1969.
 7. Collective bargaining: What is negotiable? *Am. J. Nurs.* 69:1894, 1969.
 8. *A layman's guide to basic law under the National Labor Relations Act.* Washington, D.C.: U.S. Government Printing Office, 1972. P. 2.
 9. *Ibid.*, p. 5.
10. *Ibid.*, pp. 5 and 6.
11. *Ibid.*, p. 7.
12. National Labor Relations Act jurisdiction over health care institutions. Washington, D.C.: National Labor Relations Board, 1974.

10. SOCIAL SECURITY AND THE NATIONAL HEALTH CARE PLANNING ACT

This chapter deals with several extremely complicated and important pieces of legislation. We feel compelled to warn readers again that we do not intend this book to be a definitive commentary on any piece of legislation, and, as such, a source for someone attempting to determine an individual's rights in a particular factual situation. The law is constantly changing. Statutes are amended and subject to interpretation by the courts, administrative bodies, and public officials. We have not attempted to do more than trace the broad outlines of certain legislation for the purpose of giving nurses a general conception of the scope of major laws pertaining to the health care field. We are not attempting to give them sufficient information in this text to apply the law to particular factual situations.

Perhaps no other piece of legislation growing out of the New Deal in the 1930s has had a greater impact on the lives, hopes, and aspirations of the average American than the Social Security Act of 1935. Decried by many at the time of its enactment and for decades afterward as the first step toward a socialistic society, it is now almost universally accepted in the United States. Few Americans, whether they spent their working years as unskilled laborers or as highly paid corporate executives or professionals, are too proud to claim their benefits under the Social Security Act on reaching the age of 65. Although originally designed for the primary purpose of providing some sort of income protection for wage earners after they reached the age of 65 and were compelled to leave the work force for reasons of either health or mandatory retirement age, the Act has been expanded in its purposes and coverage throughout the years.

A worker's survivors as well as certain classes of dependents of a retired worker were brought within the coverage of the Act so as to entitle them to payments under the amendments of 1939. Although originally providing coverage only for workers in industry and commerce, the Social Security Act was amended during the 1950s to bring within its coverage "most self-employed persons, most state and local employees, household and foreign employees, members of the Armed Forces and clergymen" [1]. In 1954, an amendment to the Social Security Act provided disability insurance, giving workers protection against loss of income due to total disability. In 1965, an amendment of great significance for the health care field was the Medicare Bill, which provided hospital and medical

113

insurance to people 65 and over. The Social Security Act was further amended so that from July 1, 1973, people under 65 who have been entitled to disability checks for two or more consecutive years and people with severe kidney disease requiring dialysis or kidney transplant are also entitled to such insurance benefits.

A 1972 amendment provided automatic cost of living increases in social security benefits. All of these benefits are paid from trusts funded by contributions from employers, employees, and self-employed individuals. Today, nine out of ten workers in the United States are contributing to these trust funds and nearly one out of seven Americans is receiving social security benefit checks. Almost the entire aged population of the United States, or nearly 22 million people, are protected by medicare, as are another 2.1 million disabled people under the age of 65 [2].

MEDICARE

It might be worthwhile to examine medicare more closely, since it is that aspect of the Social Security Act that has the greatest impact on the health care industry. Medicare, with its far-reaching provisions, has done a great deal to add dignity, that most precious quality, to old age. It has, to a large extent, eliminated the humiliation so common to previous generations of older Americans, who were forced to seek help from their children to pay the medical expenses of old age or else suffered the indignity of applying to free clinics and charitable institutions. For many older Americans who had raised a family and dissipated their resources by giving their children a "start in life," the cruel necessity to take charity was indeed debasing. The Social Security Act has changed most if not all of this, and Americans who have spent their lives in gainful employment need seldom fear being so totally dependent in their old age. The medicare amendment, enacted in 1965, met one of the most pressing needs caused by the rapidly spiraling trend in medical costs, which far outdistanced the capabilities of most older Americans whose incomes were either fixed or nonexistent.

Medicare's benefits may be divided into two major categories: hospital insurance, sometimes called Part A; and medical insurance, sometimes called Part B.

HOSPITAL INSURANCE

In the case of hospital insurance, medicare will pay for inpatient hospital care, inpatient care in a skilled nursing facility, and follow-up care in the home by a home health agency, subject to certain limitations and conditions.

First, the care must be reasonable and necessary, which means that it is of a kind and amount that is generally accepted as proper by the medical community for the type of medical problem that is being treated. A "utilization review committee" at each hospital and skilled nursing facility has the duty to make this determination. Professional standards review organizations perform a similar function in some parts of the country. They are composed of health care professionals who review the care prescribed by their peers to see if it meets medicare standards.

The hospital insurance provided by medicare will not cover custodial care. This is care of a nature that need not necessarily be supplied by a professionally trained individual. It involves help in bathing, dressing, eating, and taking medicine, and is care that could be supplied by any layman.

There are certain limitations on how much care can be provided under the hospital insurance provisions of medicare during each benefit period. The benefit period ends and a new one begins when a patient has been out of the hospital or a skilled nursing care facility for 60 consecutive days.

In order for medicare to pay for inpatient hospital care, all of the following standards must be met:

1. The inpatient hospital care must be prescribed by a physician for treatment of an illness or injury;

2. The care must be of a nature that can only be provided in a hospital;

3. The hospital must be one that participates in the medicare program; and

4. The treatment must not be disapproved by the utilization review committee of the hospital.

If these four standards are met, the medicare hospital insurance will pay for all covered services that are rendered in the hospital for the first 60 days, minus a $124 deductible amount for each benefit period. After the first 60 days, medicare will pay for covered services from the sixty-first through the ninetieth day, except for $31 per day. In addition, all persons covered by medicare have a 60-day lifetime reserve that they can use in any benefit period in which they run out of coverage and that will pay for inpatient hospital care charges in excess of $62 per day, if those charges are for services covered.

The types of services rendered as part of inpatient hospital care that are not covered by medicare involve personal convenience items such as radios, televisions, and telephones; extra charges for the use of a private room unless such private room is medically necessary; and the cost of private duty nurses. Also the charges for the first three pints of blood used in any benefit period are not covered [3].

During a person's lifetime, this hospital insurance will pay for no more than 190 days of care in a participating psychiatric hospital.

The hospital insurance provided by medicare will cover care in a skilled nursing facility if all of the five following standards are met:

1. The patient was in a hospital for at least 3 consecutive days before transfer to the skilled nursing facility;

2. The patient was transferred to the skilled nursing facility because he required care for the condition for which he was treated in the hospital;

3. The patient was admitted to the skilled nursing facility within a short time (generally 14 days or less) after he left the hospital;

4. A physician certified to the patient's need for skilled nursing care, and such skilled nursing care or skilled rehabilitation services were actually received by the patient on a daily basis at the skilled nursing care facility; and

5. The care provided in the skilled nursing facility was not disapproved by such facility's utilization review committee [4].

Hospitalization insurance will not cover custodial care in a skilled nursing facility. In general, it may be said that the kind of care covered in such skilled nursing facilities is that which may only be performed by or under the supervision of licensed nursing personnel or a professional therapist. Medicare covers up to 100 days' care in a skilled nursing facility during each benefit period, subject to certain conditions and restrictions. A person who leaves a skilled care nursing facility and is readmitted within 14 days does not need another 3-day stay in the hospital as a prerequisite to his readmission. During each benefit period hospital insurance under medicare pays for all covered services during the first 20 days that the patient has been in a skilled nursing facility. During the twenty-first through the hundredth day medicare will pay for all services covered, except for the first $15.50 per day, for care in a skilled nursing facility [5].

It might be added that, in general, both skilled nursing care facilities and hospitals must be participating in the medicare program in order for patients to receive medicare benefits. As in the case of inpatient hospital status, certain services in a skilled nursing care facility are not covered. Some of those services not covered by medicare are the following: personal convenience items such as televisions, radios, or telephones in the patient's room, private rooms unless needed for medical reasons, private duty nurses, and the first three pints of blood a patient receives during any one benefit period.

Some of the services actually covered in a skilled nursing care facility are as follows: the cost of a semi-private room, all meals including special diets, regular nursing service, rehabilitation services, drugs furnished by the facility, medical supplies such as splints and casts, and the use of appliances such as a wheelchair [6].

Medical Insurance
The other major category in medicare benefits is medical insurance. The

medical insurance under medicare, subject to the applicable rules and regulations, helps to pay for the following categories of medical expenses:

1. Services of physicians
2. Hospital care on outpatient basis
3. Physical therapy and speech pathology services on an outpatient basis
4. Services commonly known as home health care
5. Other health services and supplies

The benefits covered under the medical insurance portion of medicare are on a calendar-year basis rather than being governed by benefit periods such as those that govern payments under the hospitalization insurance portion of the law. As a general rule, medicare medical insurance will pay 80 percent of the expenses it covers during any calendar year, subject to an annual $60 deductible amount. This $60 deductible amount covers the entire benefit package under medical insurance and does not apply to each separate type of service covered. Stated another way, a patient need only pay $60 once in order for 80 percent reimbursement to apply to all services that he receives during one calendar year under the medical insurance portion of medicare.

PHYSICIANS' SERVICES. Subject to the $60 deductible amount, medicare medical insurance pays 80 percent of the cost of services received from a physician in his office, at the patient's home, or in a hospital. For those insured inpatients who receive radiology or pathology services from a physician, medicare medical insurance will pay 100 percent of the reasonable charges for such service, without reference to the annual deductible amount. Medical insurance will also pay 80 percent of the reasonable cost of outpatient medical treatment for mental illness; however, no more than $250 will be paid in any one year for such services. Certain types of treatment by chiropractors and podiatrists are also covered, as is dental care involving surgery of the jaw or related structures and setting of fractures of the jaw or facial bones.

In general, it may be said that, subject to certain limitations, the medical insurance portion of medicare covers medical services provided by physicians and some other health care professionals that do not involve routine physical examinations and services not generally considered essential to a patient's health. Some examples of physicians' services not covered by medical insurance are: "routine physical examinations," "routine foot care," "eye or hearing examinations for prescribing or fitting eyeglasses or hearing aids," "immunizations (unless required because of an injury or immediate risk of infection)," and "cosmetic surgery unless it is needed because of accidental injury or to improve the functioning of a malformed part of the body" [7].

OUTPATIENT HOSPITAL SERVICES. A second major category of care provided under medicare medical insurance comprises outpatient hospital services. Medicare medical insurance pays 80 percent of the cost of the reasonable charges for covered services received on an outpatient basis at a hospital, subject to the $60 annual deductible amount. Again, certain types of care, such as those previously enumerated, are not covered. Outpatient hospital services covered include the following: "services in an emergency room or outpatient clinic," "laboratory tests billed by the hospital," "x-rays and other radiology services billed by the hospital," "medical supplies such as casts, splints," and "drugs and biologicals which cannot be self-administered" [8].

OUTPATIENT PHYSICAL THERAPY AND SPEECH THERAPY SERVICES. Medicare medical insurance will pay 80 percent of the cost of medically necessary physical therapy or speech therapy, subject to the $60 annual deductible amount if such services are given in a doctor's office and included as part of the doctor's bill or are received in a participating hospital or skilled nursing facility and furnished under a plan prescribed and periodically reviewed by a physician.

If such services are received directly from an *independently practicing* medicare-certified physical therapist in his office or in the patient's home, and if such treatment is prescribed by a physician, medical insurance will pay 80 percent of the reasonable charges after the $60 deductible, up to an annual amount of payments no greater than $80.

OTHER SERVICES AND SUPPLIES COVERED BY MEDICAL INSURANCE. Medical insurance helps pay for certain types of prosthetic devices needed to substitute for an eye, limb, or internal body organ. Certain types of orthopedic braces are also covered. Dentures are not covered. Medicare medical insurance will also help pay for certain types of durable medical equipment, such as home dialysis systems and equipment that is medically necessary and prescribed by a doctor for use in the home. Various arrangements for payment can be made, whether the equipment is to be purchased or rented. In any event, medicare medical insurance usually makes monthly payments toward purchase or rental. Medicare medical insurance will help pay for diagnostic tests at laboratories certified by medicare to give the type of diagnostic procedure required. Medicare medical insurance will also help pay for ambulance transportation when the amulance service meets medicare requirements and when transportation by other means would endanger the patient's health, provided that the travel is between the patient's home and a hospital or skilled nursing facility or between the hospital and skilled nursing facility. It will also help pay for portable diagnostic x-ray services provided in the patient's home.

Home Health Care under Medicare
Medicare will pay for home health care under certain circumstances. Provisions are made for such care under both the hospital insurance and

the medical insurance sections. Medicare will pay for home health care visits involving part-time nursing care, physical therapy, and speech therapy. If any of the foregoing are required, medicare will also pay for occupational therapy, part-time services of home health aides, medical social services, and medical supplies and equipment provided in connection with such services by the supplying agency. Types of home health care that medicare will not pay for include full-time nursing at home, drugs and biologicals, meals delivered to the home, and homemaker services. Hospital insurance will pay for 100 health visits during the 12-month period following discharge from a hospital or participating skilled nursing facility when the following six conditions are met:

1. The patient was in a participating hospital for at least 3 consecutive days;

2. The home health care required by the patient is for further treatment of a condition which was treated in a hospital or skilled nursing facility;

3. The care the patient needs includes part-time skilled nursing care, physical therapy, or speech therapy;

4. The patient is confined to his or her home;

5. A doctor determined the need for home health care and set up a home health plan for the patient within 14 days after discharge from a hospital or participating skilled nursing facility; and

6. Such services are provided by a home health agency participating in medicare.

The patient does not have to submit the bills for such services, since the claims are submitted directly by the supplying agency. The medical insurance portion of medicare will also pay for up to 100 home health visits in a calendar year. Under the medical insurance portion of medicare, the patient does not have to have a 3-day stay in the hospital in order for medical insurance to pay for such home health care visits. Furthermore, the medical insurance portion will pay for home health care visits even though the 100 such visits covered by the medicare hospital insurance are already used up. Under medicare medical insurance the $60 annual deductible amount applies to home health care visits. Medicare medical insurance will pay for home health care visits if all of the following conditions are met:

1. The patient needs part-time skilled nursing care or physical or speech therapy;

2. A physician determines the need for such services and sets up the home health care plan;

3. The patient is confined to his or her home; and

4. Such services are provided by a home health care agency participating in medicare.

As in the case of home health care provided under hospitalization insurance, the patient need not send in any bills since such claims are submitted by the agency supplying the home health care services [9].

Processing of Medicare Payments

Medicare payments are processed by private insurance companies under contract with the government. In the case of claims originating in hospitals, skilled nursing facilities, and home health agencies, these processing organizations are known as *intermediaries*. The insurance companies handling the claims from doctors and other suppliers of services covered under medicare medical insurance are known as *carriers*.

REASONABLE CHARGES. All payments under the medical insurance program of medicare are limited to the *reasonable charges* for the service rendered. The reasonable charge is the customary charge or the prevailing charge, whichever is lower. The customary charge is the charge most frequently made by each doctor and supplier for each covered service furnished to patients during the previous calendar year. The prevailing charge for each service or supply is a charge that is high enough to cover the customary charges for that service or supply for 3 out of every 4 bills submitted during the previous year [10].

MEDICARE AND MEDICAID

The medicare and medicaid programs are both set up under the Social Security Act—title 18 for medicare and title 19 for medicaid. Medicare is essentially an insurance program. It is uniform throughout the United States and is supported through trust funds. It covers almost everybody over the age of 65, whether they are rich or poor. Medicaid, on the other hand, is primarily an assistance or welfare program, is funded from federal, state, and local taxes, and is in effect in 49 of the states, the exception being Arizona. It is not uniform in the places where it is in effect and is subject to variations in state law.

Details on the medicare program are available from the social security offices, whereas detailed information on the medicaid program is available from the state welfare offices. The states set their own standards for medicaid programs within federal guidelines. Medicaid can pay for charges not covered by medicare in the case of people eligible for both programs. For example, medicaid can pay the $124 deductible amount under medicare hospital insurance if the patient is eligible under both programs, and medicaid can also pay the $60 deductible under medicare medical insurance if the patient is eligible under both programs.

Under the federal guidelines, medicaid pays for at least the following services, subject to certain limitations: inpatient hospital care; outpatient hospital services; laboratory and x-ray services; skilled nursing facility care; physicians' services; screening, diagnosis, and treatment of children under 21; home health care; and family-planning services. In addition, subject to state law, it may pay for dental care, prescribed drugs, eyeglasses, clinic services, intermediate care facility services, and other diagnostic screening, preventive, and rehabilitation services [11].

However, in order to receive any of the previously mentioned benefits from medicaid the patient must be in an eligible category. In 1974, medicaid paid the bills of more than 24 million people who were aged, blind, disabled, under 21, or members of families with dependent children. Some states have set eligibility standards that include low-income people who do not fall into those categories.

Under the provisions of title VI of the Civil Rights Act of 1964,

No person in the United States shall, on the ground of race, color, or national origin, be excluded from participation in, be denied the benefit of, or be subjected to discrimination under any program or activity receiving federal financial assistance.

Since both the medicare and medicaid programs are subject to the provisions of this law, these programs have also had the effect of improving the delivery of health care services to many previously deprived groups throughout the United States [12].

NATIONAL HEALTH PLANNING AND RESOURCES DEVELOPMENT ACT OF 1974

Recognizing the inflationary trend in health care, the variations in quantity and quality of health care delivery to various segments of the population, regarding both geographical area and social economic status, and further recognizing the lack of coordinated planning in this field with input from both the consuming public and the health care providers, Congress enacted the National Health Planning and Resources Development Act of 1974 [13]. Its purpose is to facilitate the development of recommendations for national health planning policy and to authorize financial assistance in the implementation of such a policy through the development of health care resources.

The Act established an advisory council in the Department of Health, Education, and Welfare that is known as the National Council on Health Planning and Development. The council is composed of 15 members of whom not less than 5 are persons who are not providers of health care services. The Act further provides that health service areas be established throughout the United States. As a general rule, each health service area must have a population of not more than 3 million and not less than 500,000.

Each health service area must have a health systems agency, which can be a nonprofit private corporation, a public regional planning body, or a single unit of general local government. The health systems agency has the power and funding to maintain a staff to implement the following 10 health priorities set forth in the National Health Planning Act:

(1) Primary care for medically underserved populations.
(2) Multi-institutional coordination or consolidation of services.
(3) Medical group practices (health maintenance organizations).
(4) Training in utilization of physician assistance.
(5) Multi-institutional sharing of support services.
(6) Improvement in the quality of health services.
(7) Institutional capacity to provide various levels of care.
(8) Promotion of health.
(9) Uniform cost accounting, reimbursement, utilization reporting, and management procedures.
(10) Public education [14].

Each health systems agency develops a health systems plan (HSP), which, pursuant to the 10 priorities set forth in the Act, constitutes a detailed statement of goals. Before establishing an HSP, the health systems agency holds hearings and gives interested parties a chance to submit their views both orally and in writing. Once the HSP has been adopted, the agencies establish an annual review and amend as necessary an annual implementation plan to achieve the goals of the HSP. This annual implementation plan (AIP) also sets priorities appropriate to the particular health service area.

State Health Planning and Development
The National Health Planning and Resources Development Act provides for coordination of the health service areas within each state by means of statewide organizations known as state health planning and development agencies. Each state health planning and development agency is governed by a council known as the statewide health coordinating council, roughly analogous to the health systems agency. It promulgates and implements a state administrative program, which coordinates and implements the various health service plans promulgated by the health service areas and health systems agencies within the state's borders. The council consists of no fewer than 16 members, with each health systems agency within the borders of the state having at least two representatives. Not less than half of the representatives of each health systems agency are consumers rather than health care providers.

Subject to applicable regulations, the Secretary of the Department of Health, Education, and Welfare makes grants to state health planning and development agencies to assist them in meeting the costs of their operation.

Centers for Health Planning
The Act provides for at least 5 health planning service centers to be in operation by June 30, 1976. These centers shall provide

technical and consulting assistance as health systems agencies and State Agencies may from time to time require, conducting research, studies and analysis of health planning and resources development, and developing health planning approaches, methodologies, policies and standards . . . [15].

For the purposes of establishing and operating the health planning service centers the following standards will apply:

There are authorized to be appropriated 5 million dollars for the fiscal year ending June 30, 1975, 8 million dollars for the fiscal year ending June 30, 1976, and 10 million dollars for the fiscal year ending June 30, 1977 [16].

While the goals of the National Health Planning and Resources Development Act of 1974 cannot be classified as anything less than praiseworthy, in our opinion this complex and comprehensive piece of legislation will prove to be a national disaster from a practical point of view. In an era when the country is trying to unburden itself from the cost of "big government," the Act sets up an expensive and complex new organization out of which many bureaucratic empires undoubtedly will be built. The wording of the Act, while seemingly detailed, will offer ample leeway for professional "grantsmen" who will have the opportunity to found innumerable administrative hierarchies throughout the nation bearing a questionable relationship to the actual health and well-being of its citizens. Although this law is intended to replace several health programs presently in operation, it seems to have done so by creating a bigger and more complex bureaucracy than all the others combined. The only restraint on this many-headed monster will be the willingness of Congress to appropriate money. Perhaps with time and experience Congress will amend the Act and simplify the structure of its national health planning organization in such a way as to give the public more actual health care for its tax dollar. Unfortunately, in respect to this possibility, we are somewhat pessimistic.

REFERENCES
1. *Your social security.* U.S. Department of Health, Education, and Welfare, Social Security Administration. DHEW Publication No. (SSA) 76-10035, January 1976. P. 5.
2. *Ibid.*, pp. 5, 6.
3. *Your medicare handbook.* U.S. Department of Health, Education, and Welfare, Social Security Administration. DHEW Publication No. (SSA) 76-10050, January 1976. Pp. 12-14.
4. *Ibid.*, p. 17.
5. *Ibid.*, p. 18.
6. *Ibid.*, p. 19.
7. *Ibid.*, p. 27.
8. *Ibid.*, p. 29.

9. *Ibid.*, p. 37.
10. *Ibid.*, p. 21.
11. *Medicaid medicare which is which?* Medical Services Administration Social and Rehabilitation Service, United States Department of Health, Education, and Welfare. DHEW Publication No. (SRS) 75;24902, 1975. P. 15.
12. *Ibid.*, p. 28.
13. Public Law 93-641, 93rd Congress, S. 2994, January 5, 1975.
14. Regional Health Line, Regional Comprehensive Planning Council, Inc., Philadelphia. Vol. 1, No. 6, Special Edition, 1975. P. 1.
15. Public Law 93-641, section 1534(a).
16. Public Law 93-641, section 1534(d).

11. DEATH

Birth and death are the two most truly universal experiences of mankind. While we are eager to unravel the mysteries surrounding the creation of human beings from the moment of conception to birth, there is a perceptible hesitation on the part of physicians, philosophers, sociologists, legislators, judges, and lawyers to study and understand the physiological process known as death and to attempt to determine what legal principles apply at life's final moment.

Because of recent advances in medical science which make possible the preservation of some form of life in the face of catastrophic illness or trauma, and because of the newly found ability of medical science to transplant human organs, the legal profession is now faced with the task of reexamining death to determine when it actually occurs.

With the ability to preserve life there has arisen a corresponding ability to prolong suffering and to extend a form of existence that may not truly be classified as life. Again, this has presented the legislatures and the legal profession with new problems. When, if ever, is it permissible to terminate the existence of an individual in great and intractable pain, or an individual whose brain has been damaged to the extent that he has permanently lost the ability to respond to his environment? At the present time it may be said that these problems have not been resolved in terms of universally applied principles. Different forums and jurisdictions have applied varying rules and standards.

EUTHANASIA

Literally translated, euthanasia means "good death." In the minds of the public, the word is synonymous with *mercy killing*. The word *euthanasia* implies an active role on the part of someone to hasten the death of another. It may be distinguished from the commonly used phrase "death with dignity," which refers to a passive failure or omission to prolong life [1,2].

Under the English common law there was no civil liability for the death of another; however, such a liability was created in Parliament in 1846 by Lord Campbell's Act, which imposed pecuniary liability on one who caused a wrongful death. Lord Campbell's Act was the predecessor of the *wrongful death statutes*, in effect throughout the United States, that impose civil liability on one who causes the wrongful death of another. Typically, under these acts the heirs of the decedent have a cause of action for money damages against the wrongdoer.

It is under these wrongful death statutes that a physician faces potential civil liability for his role in a patient's death. It must be said as a general rule that deliberately shortening or terminating the life of another, even though done for humane reasons to a person who is terminally ill and suffering from intractable pain, is illegal and the actor is subject to liability for money damages under a wrongful death statute.

Although not specifically set forth in any applicable law, it is the practice of courts, juries, and society in general to make a distinction between passive and active euthanasia as well as between voluntary and involuntary euthanasia. Furthermore, certain considerations apply when an individual's religious scruples prohibit him from accepting certain types of medical treatment that are designed to prolong or save a life. The case of an incompetent patient presents special problems in making decisions regarding appropriate means for the prolongation of life in the face of a terminal illness.

The majority rule is that the consent of a patient to an act or omission that would shorten or terminate the patient's life is no defense to a physician and this rule applies even when the patient actively solicits such an act or omission to end the intractable pain of a terminal illness [3]. Many writers in this field have indicated that a physician has a moral and professional duty to accede to such requests if he feels they are morally justified. In effect, those writers are telling physicians to do what they think is right and accept the legal consequences of their acts even at a time when the law in this field is still in a nebulous and developing stage and these legal consequences are far from uniform or predictable.

The Religious Exception

An exception to the majority rule that life must be preserved in all circumstances is the "religious exception." The first amendment of the United States Constitution forbids any law prohibiting the free exercise of religion. Recognizing the prohibitions of the first amendment, the courts have refused to order medical treatment to preserve life when it is refused by a patient on religious grounds. Cases involving Jehovah's Witnesses who refuse blood transfusions frequently appear in the newspapers. When the patient is a competent adult, the courts have generally refused to order a blood transfusion or other lifesaving measure in the face of a religious objection.

As is the case with many legal principles, there are several exceptions to the exception. The courts have generally disregarded the prohibition of the first amendment and ordered medical treatment in the face of religious objections in cases in which there was a significant public interest in health, safety, and welfare involved. For example, in the case of compulsory vaccination, the interest of the public in preventing epidemics overrides the rights guaranteed by the first amendment, and the court will order that vaccinations be carried out even in the face of religious objections.

Another exception is for minors and mental incompetents. Even though the parents of a child or the guardian of an incompetent object to medical treatment on religious grounds for such child or incompetent, the courts will generally order the treatment in spite of first amendment rights to the contrary.

In the case of *John F. Kennedy Memorial Hospital v. Heston*, a patient was admitted to a hospital suffering from a ruptured spleen. When the patient first entered the hospital she was in shock and opposition to a transfusion was expressed by her mother, who signed a release of liability to the hospital and medical personnel. On application by the hospital, a guardian was appointed with authority to consent to the blood transfusion. The patient herself later sought to have the order appointing the guardian set aside, but the Supreme Court of New Jersey upheld the lower court's refusal to set aside the order appointing the guardian on the grounds that the state has a compelling interest in preserving the life of its citizens and that "... there is no constitutional right to choose to die...." [4]. This case probably sets forth a minority point of view, since a number of other cases have upheld the right of a patient to refuse lifesaving treatment on religious grounds.

A case expressing the majority view, *In re Osbourne*, involved a 34-year-old man who was suffering from internal bleeding when admitted to the hospital. He refused to consent to a transfusion and his wife also refused to consent, both refusals being on religious grounds. An appellate court held that there was an insufficient state interest to warrant overriding individual desires based on religious beliefs and reversed a lower court order granting the hospital's petition for a guardian. The court in this case specifically rejected the principle of the Heston case that there is an overriding state interest in preserving life [5].

An interesting philosophical problem arises from these cases, since most of the cases based on religious exception involve patients who may be returned to a normal or an almost normal life by the administration of blood transfusions or other health care measures. If the majority of courts believe that the patient has the right to refuse medical treatment that would return him to a normal life, why should not a patient with a terminal illness be allowed the same choice, when accepting treatment in his case would only prolong a life filled with pain [6].

How then should this question affect nurses? Certainly a nurse may be joined with the treating physician, the hospital, and other medical personnel in a lawsuit by a patient for assault and battery and invasion of privacy in a case in which lifesaving treatment is given over the patient's objection and without a court order.

Another aspect of the dilemma is that health care personnel who withhold life-preserving treatment at a patient's request may also be subject to civil action for wrongful death or a criminal action for homicide. Because of her role, in most hospitals it is more likely that a nurse would be involved in administering care to a patient who did not want it than that she would make a unilateral decision to withhold treatment at the patient's request. She might accede to the patient's request, either on her own initiative or in following the orders of a physician or other superior. It is doubtful whether even a broad form professional liability policy would offer a nurse protection from civil liability in such a case.

Passive Euthanasia

A physician or nurse who terminates or shortens the life of a terminally ill patient by a deliberate and willful act is obviously subject to criminal and civil liability. The issue of liability becomes somewhat clouded when we substitute for the willful and deliberate act an intentional omission or failure to give life-preserving or life-lengthening therapy to the same terminally ill patient. Causing the death of a terminally ill patient by failure to give the therapy necessary to extend life has been called passive euthanasia. According to Percy Foreman, such passive euthanasia will impose criminal liability on the health care personnel responsible for the terminally ill patient's care if there was a legal duty to the patient to provide such care [7].

The Supreme Court of Michigan held in *People v. Beardsley* that it must be ". . . a legal duty, and not a mere moral obligation. It must be a duty imposed by law or by contract, and the omission to perform the duty must be the immediate and direct cause of death" [8]. If a physician or a nurse undertakes the care of a patient, that physician or nurse has a legal obligation to continue such care as long as the case requires. Of course, this obligation or duty may be terminated by the discharge of the health care professional involved or by the death of the patient. In fact, this legal obligation is frequently disregarded, with no penalty, civil or criminal, imposed on the physician or nurse involved. One of the most frequent instances is in the case of deformed infants who are allowed to die when medical procedures are readily available to prolong their lives. Frequently life-supporting measures are also withheld from terminally ill patients in intractable pain.

Although the law is clear that civil and criminal liability attach to the physician or nurse involved, at least for withholding ordinary care, there are few if any recorded cases in which such sanctions have been imposed. In the case of passive euthanasia, complex legal issues frequently arise. One involves the question of what is active and what is passive euthanasia. Does the doctor who turns off the respirator perform a positive act or is such pulling of the plug merely an omission and passive. This issue has not been resolved by the courts. Certainly it is passive euthanasia or an omission to withhold the use of a respirator if it has never been turned on in the first place. But the problem becomes crucial for a physician when extraordinary measures such as the use of a respirator are applied to a patient who is seriously injured before the extent of brain damage is known.

Another issue frequently confronted by physicians treating terminally ill patients or deformed children is the differentiation between ordinary treatment and extraordinary treatment. One may distinguish ordinary and extraordinary care by saying that ordinary treatment includes medical or surgical treatment that does not involve excessive discomfort or expense and provides a reasonable possibility of benefiting the patient. Conversely, extraordinary treatment offers the patient no reasonable possibility of improving his condition and does subject him to excessive discomfort or expense [7].

The use of a respirator is certainly extraordinary care for a patient with no hope of regaining spontaneous respiration. There is certainly no legal obligation to use or continue to use a respirator on a patient who is already dead; however, the issue of when death actually occurs has not been completely and uniformly resolved by the courts. In short, although passive euthanasia is widely practiced by physicians and nurses, legal sanctions have rarely been imposed by the courts. However, it appears that the physicians, nurses, and other health care personnel practicing such passive euthanasia have in fact exposed themselves to civil and criminal liability. It must therefore remain largely a professional, moral, and ethical decision for those actually involved until such time as the courts and legislatures come to grips with the problem and set appropriate standards that they are willing to enforce actively. It is an area in which we decline to take a position or make any recommendations.

Active Euthanasia

Active euthanasia is perhaps synonymous with the generally accepted definition of euthanasia itself. It involves a deliberate act by a physician, nurse, or other person to shorten or terminate the life of a terminally ill patient. It must be distinguished from aiding and abetting a suicide, which involves aiding or providing the means by which a terminally ill patient can end his own life.

For example, one who supplied poison to a terminally ill patient who desired to terminate his life would be guilty, at most, of aiding and abetting a suicide, whereas one who actually placed the poison in the patient's mouth or otherwise administered it to him would be guilty of murder.

In some states, such as Texas, no criminal liability attaches to aiding and abetting a suicide, since suicide itself is not a crime. Under English common law it was a crime and according to Blackstone, it was a double offense.

One spiritual, and invading the prerogative of the Almighty; the other temporal, against the king who hath interest in the preservation of all his subjects . . . [9].

Voluntary Euthanasia

The act of euthanasia may be voluntary or involuntary, that is to say, in the case of voluntary euthanasia a terminally ill patient will ask the physician or other health care professional taking care of him to terminate or shorten his life. This can be done by a deliberate act, such as administering a lethal drug, or passively by omitting life-preserving treatment. In either case, in most jurisdictions, the physician, nurse, or other health care professional involved would be guilty of criminal homicide and also subject to civil liability for wrongful death. This type of euthanasia has been widely practiced in the past and with the growth of the concept of "death with dignity" and the proliferation of "living wills," we may expect to see voluntary euthanasia become even more prevalent.

A living will is a testament by a mentally competent individual expressing his desire that he not be kept alive by extraordinary or even ordinary means when he is suffering intractable pain from a terminal illness from which recovery is impossible. Typically, the living will authorizes the administration of drugs to relieve pain even if they will shorten life. It may be revoked by the person making it at any time as long as he is mentally competent.

This type of will is usually carried on an individual's person and also given to his lawyer, spouse, and physician. It is generally executed prior to the onset of the terminal illness but may be executed at any time while a person is mentally competent. Such living wills and other expressions of desire for death do not relieve the person causing the death from criminal or civil liability except under very limited circumstances in California. However, we are again faced with the discrepancy between that which the law provides and the way the law is actually implemented. There are few prosecutions for euthanasia, whether active or passive. Of course, this does not ensure a physician or nurse freedom from liability if he or she participates in such acts, but it does point out the need for farsighted legislation in this field. It should set realistic standards and guidelines that are in accord with current moral and ethical beliefs. Even in the case of involuntary euthanasia, which is euthanasia practiced without the consent of the patient, who is frequently incompetent due to a comatose state, prosecutions are infrequent so long as the motive is apparently humanitarian [10].

Involuntary Euthanasia

In the case of a terminally ill patient who is incompetent, whether such incompetency is caused by minority, mental disease, or a comatose state, a physician or nurse who practices euthanasia, whether actively or passively, is subject to criminal liability for homicide under a strict construction of the law. Again we are faced with the dilemma that we previously discussed, namely, that the law provides for a punishment for certain acts such as euthanasia but that punishment is rarely, if ever, applied by courts and juries if the motive of the person performing euthanasia is apparently humanitarian.

As to the civil liability of the nurse or doctor involved in euthanasia of a mentally incompetent person, the situation is not quite so clear. Certainly, an incompetent person is not capable of giving a valid consent to either active or passive euthanasia. It is true that such an individual could have given his consent at a time when he had full legal capacity by making a living will, the terms of which have been described previously. Such a document would be automatically revoked if a testator became incompetent from a condition not contemplated at the time he executed the living will; otherwise, it would remain in effect even though the testator later became incompetent or entered a comatose state. Under the law in its present state, such a document would offer no protection to a nurse or physician who committed an act of euthanasia. However, some changes are currently contemplated in the laws of California. It might even be argued that a living will goes against public policy inasmuch as it condones criminal homicide.

It could be argued that if all of the heirs of a terminally ill and legally incompetent patient were legally competent and signed properly drafted consent forms, it is probable, but not certain, that they, at least, would thereby be prevented from later bringing a civil action for wrongful death. It must be pointed out, however, that no matter what precautions a physician or nurse takes before committing an act of euthanasia, the risk of civil or criminal liability cannot be totally eliminated under the law in its present stage of development. Some individuals feel that the moral and ethical considerations involved outweigh the potential risk of liability, but this is certainly a highly personal decision. Again, it is an area in which we ourselves decline to take a position or make any recommendations [11, 12].

THE RIGHT TO BE LET ALONE

A natural extension to the rule which allows a patient to refuse lifesaving treatment on religious grounds by virtue of the first amendment to the Federal Constitution is the right to be let alone. The right to be let alone means simply that a person, within very broad limits, has a right to control his own destiny and to do with his possessions and his body what he wishes. The patient's wishes need not be based on traditional religious views, but may be based on his own desires and opinions, whether or not they are of religious origin and whether or not they conform to those prevailing in society. The only requirement is that the patient be legally competent to make a decision.

In 1964, Justice Warren Burger based his dissenting opinion in the *Georgetown College* case on the right to be let alone. In that case, a blood transfusion was required to save a patient's life and was refused by the patient and her husband on religious grounds. The court ordered that the blood transfusion be given on the grounds that it was "obvious that the woman was not in a mental condition to make a decision." Justice Burger held in his dissent that

This episode presents on the one hand an example of a grave dilemma which confronts those who engage in the healing arts and on the other hand some very basic and fundamental issues on the nature and scope of judicial power. We can sympathize with the one but we cannot safely or appropriately temporize with the other; we have an obligation to deal with the basic question whether any judicially cognizable issue is presented when a legally competent adult refuses, on grounds of conscience, to consent to a medical treatment essential to preserve life. The end, desirable as it obviously developed, cannot establish the existence of a case or controversy if such did not exist independent of the sequel to the enforced medical treatment [13].

According to Justice Burger, the real issue in the Georgetown case was whether the hospital that was petitioning the court for an order to give the lifesaving blood transfusion had a legally recognized and protected right to give such treatment. Certainly, as Justice Burger pointed out in the balance of his opinion, the hospital could not be sued because the patient and her husband had both volunteered to sign a waiver to relieve the hospital of any liability. Hence, there was no legally protected right of the hospital that the court was obliged to enforce, and the patient had not invaded any legal right of the hospital by refusing treatment. Justice Burger also held that the right to be let alone is broader than any concept of religion and should be granted to all people, no matter what their religion.

An analogous situation arose during the Viet Nam War when the Supreme Court held, in a case regarding the draft, that the right to be a conscientious objector could not be restricted to those whose objection was based on religious grounds.

UNENUMERATED RIGHTS UNDER
THE NINTH AMENDMENT

The ninth amendment to the Federal Constitution, adopted in 1791, provides that "The enumeration in the Constitution, of certain rights, shall not be construed to deny or disparage others retained by the people."

The purpose of the ninth amendment was to introduce flexibility into the Constitution. It was to ensure that the rights specifically listed in the Constitution would not be considered exclusive and preclude the enforcement of other natural and fundamental rights that were part of the traditions and collective conscience of the American people.

Patterson suggested in *The Forgotten 9th Amendment* that the ninth amendment was prospective in nature and encompassed not only rights that existed at the time it was adopted in 1791, but also others which would be recognized in the future. Hence, rights that were certainly not contemplated by the framers of the Constitution, such as the right of a couple to practice contraception, the right of a woman to have an abortion, and the right to die, all may be considered unenumerated rights protected by the ninth amendment.

Recently the rights involved in contraception and abortion have been recognized in court decisions. It cannot be long until the courts are forced to come to grips with the right to die, which certainly appears to be a fundamental right that is part of the tradition and conscience of the people, and that is demonstrated by the wide practice of various forms of euthanasia in this country [14].

DEATH DEFINED

Death, that universally anticipated experience, has received its most widely accepted definition from *Black's Law Dictionary*, which states that death is

The cessation of life; the ceasing to exist; defined by physicians as a total stoppage of the circulation of the blood, and a cessation of the animal and vital functions consequent thereon, such as respiration, pulsation, etc. . . . [15].

Up to the present time the definition in *Black's Law Dictionary* has been the one most widely relied on by courts in the United States when deciding issues involving the time of death. This view of death, based on the irreversible cessation of the vital functions of respiration, circulation, and pulsation, is the traditional view of death. It has been restated in various ways in various courts, at times somewhat redundantly as in the case of *Sanger v. Butler*, in which a Texas court interpreted a will containing the phrase "in the case of the death of my wife, Mary Butler, and myself at the same time." Here the court held that

Doubtless the word "death", in the majority of instances in which it is ordinarily employed, means "the act of dying". This, however, we regard as restrictive meaning. In its broader sense, the word "death" imports "the state or condition of being dead" [16].

A Missouri court was guilty of the same sort of redundancy in the case of *Fitch v. Edwards*, in which it was held that death meant "departure from life" [17].

Although people are dying today in precisely the same way they always have, death itself not having changed, a new definition and method of determination of the actual moment of death are required as a result of advances in medical science and the complexities of modern society. We now know that death is a continuum and that different parts of the body die at different times. The central nervous system is very vulnerable to oxygen deprivation, and brain cells may be irreversibly damaged or die while the respiratory or the circulatory system is still capable of resuscitation. Because of the development of the respirator and other medical devices, it is possible to prolong the respiration, circulation, and pulsation in an individual whose brain is irreversibly damaged.

Developments in the field of organ transplants have made a new definition of death an absolute necessity, and surgeons who remove a vital organ from a body that is still breathing and pulsating can be technically guilty of homicide under the traditional definition of death. A lawyer defending the attacker of a person whose brain was destroyed by an unlawful assault and whose heart was then donated to another patient can claim that the victim was murdered by the doctor who removed his heart rather than by the assailant who hit him over the head. Beneficiaries of double-indemnity life insurance policies may fail to collect under the accidental death provision if the person insured is kept alive by a respirator for more than one year after the injury, even though brain activity has long since stopped.

These and other problems necessitate the search for a new definition of death. The broad framework into which the new definition fits is human potential. The human body without the potential to interact with its environment or with other persons, or to respond to stimuli, must be considered no longer a part of humanity, and therefore dead. The method of determining that this human potential has disappeared and that its disappearance is truly irreversible is, of course, the issue.

It is almost universally accepted that a person's human potential lies in his central nervous system. It is reasonable to say that when the brain dies or is destroyed the person has died or been destroyed. Therefore, the diagnostic tool which is crucial to determining the existence of human potential in a body that is still breathing and pulsating is the electroencephalogram (EEG). With certain exceptions, a flat or isoelectronic EEG indicates that the human potential of a body has disappeared and ceased to exist. There have been cases in which brain activity has returned after a flat EEG, especially when the individual has been treated with certain types of drugs and has been subjected to hypothermia. The longer the EEG remains flat, the more likely that loss of human potential is permanent and that the individual's brain is dead.

In the field of organ transplants, the conflict of interest between the potential donor and the donee is apparent. It is, of course, in the interest of the potential donor and his family that there be absolute certainty that loss of brain activity is permanent. The longer a flat EEG persists, the greater the certainty becomes. The interest of the recipient may be in direct opposition to that of the donor; he may be in critical condition and in desperate and immediate need of an organ transplant to survive. Furthermore, the longer a potential donor remains on a respirator and subject to artificial support or therapy, the more likely it is that the transplanted organ will be damaged and unable to function in its recipient.

It is generally accepted that the interest of the donor in not having his organs removed until his death is truly irreversible is paramount. Various safeguards have been adopted by the medical profession to achieve this end. In most hospitals it is required that the donor and donee be cared for by different physicians in an effort to avoid a conflict of interest. Different criteria have been set up for the time for which a flat or isoelectronic EEG must persist before an individual is considered dead.

According to a Swedish study, loss of brain function is divided into three stages: "(1) *Soper*, with reflex functions maintained; these are the cases where maintenance of medical care can lead to recovery even after months; (2) *Coma*, in which there is loss of muscletonus, poor brain reflexes with reduced function of respiratory, vasomotor and tempera-ture-regulating centers; here recovery is again possible; (3) *Abolished brain function*" [18]. The last is synonymous with death and persists for about an hour.

Dr. Roy Cohen of Stanford University proposed an EEG that remains flat for 48 hours as a reasonable criterion for death [19].

According to Dr. Gunnar Biorck of Sweden, the cerebral cortical cells that are involved in the higher brain functions are most sensitive to the arrest of circulation. They begin to die within 5 minutes after circulation is terminated. Within 15 minutes after total cessation of circulation, the whole brain may be considered irreversibly dead [20].

The first step forward from the traditional view of death seems to be the concept of brain death, which involves the total lack of activity in all parts of the brain and a resulting isoelectronic, or flat, EEG. A view that is more enlightened, at least in our opinion, would define death in terms of de-struction of the cerebrum. The medula, cerebellum, and midbrain may produce spontaneous circulation and respiration in the absence of a functioning cerebrum, but without consciousness, awareness, or true human potential. A person whose cerebrum has ceased to function has truly ended his existence as a member of humanity and is no longer able to interact with other people or respond to his environment.

Baylor University Medical Center in Dallas is considering the following definition of death based on cessation of cerebral activity for cases in which organ transplant is being considered:

For determining death in patients whose bodily functions continue with the aid of artificial support, the following criteria will govern:
(a) There will be no perceptible signs of mental awareness of environment or external stimulation, and the patient shall be unable to maintain, without artificial support, one or more vital bodily functions essential to recovery and maintenance of consciousness as described.
(b) The above described state shall be a permanent and irreversible cerebral state, or the condition causing such state shall be irreversible, precluding any reasonable expectation of patient recovery.
(c) Physician or physicians making such determination of death will employ resources of examination, observation, and such tests and consultations as may be appropriate to this determination. The merit of consultation in this inherently grave determination is self-evident [21].

In summary, it appears from the available literature in this field that medical and legal thinking is slowly developing toward acceptance of the concept of cerebral death. Although a definition of death resting solely on destruction of the cerebrum may require more sophisticated evaluation than that based on the brain-death concept or the traditional view of death based on cessation of respiration and circulation, it seems to be the only concept truly in accord with modern moral and ethical thinking, which holds that the moment of death is the moment when a person has finally and irreversibly lost his potential to respond to other human beings and to his environment.

TORT AND CRIMINAL LIABILITY IN ORGAN TRANSPLANTS

The courts have lagged behind the medical profession in accepting the concepts of brain death and cerebral death. However, as in the field of euthanasia, there is a discrepancy between the law that exists and the law that is applied.

There is also a total lack of uniformity throughout the 50 states with regard to the definition of death. In general, it may be said that, regardless of the actual state of the law, physicians have not been subjected to criminal charges for removing a vital organ from an individual with a flat EEG. In regard to civil liability, a physician who removes a vital organ from an individual with a flat EEG may still be the target of wrongful death action. This possibility is reduced somewhat if a physician receives the written consent from all of the donor's statutory heirs and if all these heirs are of age and legally competent to give such consent. In practice, organ transplant surgery is widely used throughout the United States and, in most cases, without civil or criminal actions being brought against the physicians and nurses involved. However, in view of the presently developing and still unsettled state of the law in this field, we cannot assure physicians and nurses participating in these operations that they do so with complete immunity from civil or criminal liability [22, 23, 24].

The Commission on Medical Malpractice of the Secretary of Health, Education, and Welfare found that "the question of the legal definition of death is of such importance that the definition should be enacted into law only by the Congress of the United States" [25]. While we agree that there is need for a uniform definition of death, we doubt that enactment of such a law by Congress would be constitutional.

APPARENT TRENDS
Statutes and Case Law
There is an apparent trend in the United States to redefine death so that under certain circumstances the traditional view involving the cessation of respiration, circulation, and pulsation is replaced by the definition involving brain death or even cerebral death. While most of the courts throughout the United States still apply the traditional definition of death, the process of redefinition and the adoption of the brain death or cerebral death standard is steadily proceeding on two parallel paths in this country.

One path is statutory redefinition. Six states have, by statute, defined death in terms of irreversible cessation of brain activity. The statute adopted by Kansas in 1971 is typical.

DEFINITION OF DEATH. A person will be considered medically and legally dead if, in the opinion of a physician, based on ordinary standards of medical practice, there is the absence of spontaneous respiratory and cardiac function and, because of the disease or condition which caused, directly or indirectly, these functions to cease, or because of the passage of time since these functions ceased, attempts at resuscitation are considered hopeless; and, in this event, death shall have occurred at the time these functions ceased; or

A person will be considered medically and legally dead if, in the opinion of a physician, based on ordinary standards of medical practice, there is the absence of spontaneous brain function; and if based on ordinary standards of medical practice, during reasonable attempts to either maintain or restore spontaneous circulatory or respiratory function in the absence of aforesaid brain function, it appears that further attempts at resuscitation or supportive maintenance will not succeed, death will have occurred at the time when these conditions first coincide. Death is to be pronounced before artificial means of supporting respiratory and circulatory function are terminated and before any vital organ is removed for purposes of transplantation.

These alternative definitions of death are to be utilized for all purposes in this state, including the trials of civil and criminal cases, any laws to the contrary notwithstanding [26].

The Kansas statute defines death in alternative terms, giving a choice of either brain death or the traditional standard. Maryland and Virginia have followed the lead of Kansas in this regard.

The California Health and Safety Code in section 7180 states that

A person shall be pronounced dead if it is determined by a physician that the person has suffered a total and irreversible cessation of brain function. There shall be independent confirmation of the death by another physician.

Nothing in this chapter shall prohibit a physician from using other usual and customary procedures for determining death as the exclusive basis for pronouncing a person dead [27].

The California statute therefore avoids the alternative definitions of death and instead relies on different procedures for determination of one phenomenon, the end of human life [28].

While the statutory approach to the definition of death has been criticized as being too rigid, this has not in fact been the case, since the statutes involved have used terms such as *ordinary medical standards*, which allow flexibility and conformity with current medical practice.

Another advantage of the statutory approach is the great opportunity for public involvement in framing statutes. It eliminates the uncertainty and consequent mental anguish involved in defining law by litigation.

Notwithstanding all the advantages of the statutory approach, the definition process has also been proceeding in the courts through the case law approach [29]. A landmark case in the field, *State v. Brown*, was decided in Oregon in 1971. In that case, a defendant appealed his second-degree murder conviction on the basis that the victim had not died by the gunshot wound that the defendant had inflicted and that had destroyed the vital centers of the victim's brain. Rather, the defendant contended that death was caused by the attending physician who removed the devices that were artificially supporting respiration and circulation. The Oregon court rejected the defendant's argument and ruled that death was inflicted by the gunshot wound that caused brain death and not by the subsequent removal of the supportive aids. This was the first major decision accepting the brain death standard [30].

In 1972, a Virginia court in the case of *Tucker's Administrator v. Lower* [31] recognized brain death as an alternative standard available to the jury, along with the traditional definition of death, in determining the actual time that death occurred. In that case the plaintiff brought a wrongful death action against the members of the transplant team at the Medical College of Virginia, alleging that they had removed his brother's heart before death had occurred. The evidence indicated that the brother had sustained an irreversible loss of brain function at the time he was taken to the operating room, but that he had exhibited normal body temperature, pulse, respiration, and blood pressure. In his instructions to the jury, the judge offered the alternative of determining the time of death on the basis of brain death or on the basis of the traditional standard. The jury, in returning a verdict for the defendant, adopted brain death as the proper standard. It may be argued that the court should choose the correct standard and not leave this option to the jury.

In any event, standards are still far from uniform throughout the United States in this rapidly evolving field of law. Nurses and physicians should be aware that, although the imposition of sanctions may be remote, the law is still unsettled in regard to time of death. As participants in heart transplant operations and other procedures involving the removal of vital organs, they may be required to defend their actions in court.

The Karen Quinlan Case
Perhaps no case involving the termination of extraordinary life-support measures for terminally ill patients has received as much interest and publicity in the United States as the case involving Karen Quinlan [32]. This case involved a young woman who received severe and irreversible brain damage that reduced her to a vegetative condition with no hope of returning to a cognitive, sapient state. While the destructive forces that damaged Miss Quinlan's brain did not do so to the extent necessary for her to meet the criteria for brain death, she appeared to have no chance of enjoying life in the future on other than a vegetative level.

When she was first brought to the hospital after her collapse, she was placed on a respirator and her attending physicians believed that she would live only a short time if it were removed. Since she continued to manifest a minor amount of brain activity, her attending physicians believed they would not be justified in removing the respirator without court approval. Miss Quinlan's father petitioned the chancery division of the Superior Court of New Jersey requesting that he be appointed guardian of his daughter, with authority to order the discontinuance of all extraordinary medical procedures sustaining her life. This petition was refused and an appeal was taken to the Supreme Court of New Jersey, before which the case was argued on January 26, 1976. The Supreme Court rendered its decision on March 31 of the same year. Its opinion, delivered by its chief justice, will be binding in the State of New Jersey and persuasive throughout the rest of the United States.

The Supreme Court of New Jersey held that the father of Karen Quinlan had a sufficient legal interest in the matter to make him a proper party to the litigation. The court found, in effect, that it was proper for the father to act on behalf of the daughter since she was not competent. It found that Karen Quinlan would probably have asked for discontinuance of the life-support systems if she ". . . were herself miraculously lucid for an interval (not altering the existing prognosis of the condition to which she would soon return) and perceptive of her irreversible condition . . ." and that it would be proper for her to do so even if such action meant ". . . the prospect of natural death" [32]. The court found that to hold otherwise would be to deprive Karen Quinlan of her constitutionally protected right of privacy, and it was on the basis of this right of privacy that the case was ultimately decided.

The court ordered the appointment of Karen Quinlan's father as her guardian, with the express provision that he had the right to authorize discontinuance of extraordinary life-support measures with the concurrence of her family, the attending physicians, who might be chosen by the father, and the hospital ethics committee of the institution in which Karen Quinlan was hospitalized. The opinion further provided that such concurrence by the ethics committee and the attending physicians must be based on their finding ". . . that there is no reasonable possibility of Karen's ever emerging from her present comatose condition to a cognitive, sapient state. . ." [32]. The Court ruled that if these conditions were met, withdrawal of the present life-support systems would be without criminal or civil liability on any of the participants in such withdrawal. The court further expressly provided that the applicability of its decision was not limited to cases in which there is a permanent loss of cognitive or sapient function. Furthermore the decision did not imply that there was a necessity for resort to the courts for every implementation of the opinion in comparable situations.

Certainly, this opinion greatly clarifies the law in regard to withdrawal of extraordinary life-support systems in the state of New Jersey. Until the highest courts of other states act in this area, the Quinlan opinion will be of great persuasive effect in other jurisdictions as well.

REFERENCES
1. Sharp, Thomas H., Jr., and Crofts, Thomas H., Jr. Death with dignity—The physician's civil liability. *Baylor Law Rev.* 27:8, 1975.
2. Compton, A. Christian. Telling the time of death by statute: An essential and progressive trend. *Washington and Lee Law Rev.* 31:528, 1974.
3. Malone, Robert J. Is there a right to a natural death? *N. Engl. Law Rev.* 9:293, 1974.
4. John F. Kennedy Memorial Hospital v. Heston. 58 N.J. 576 (1971).

5. In re Osbourne. 294 A2d 372 (D.C. App. 1972).

6. Malone, pp. 297-303.

7. Foreman, Percy. The physician's criminal liability for the practice of euthanasia. *Baylor Law Rev.* 27:57, 1975.

8. People v. Beardsley. 150 Mich. 206 (1907).

9. Foreman, p. 59.

10. Kutner, Luis. The living will—Coping with the historical event of death. *Baylor Law Rev.* 27:37, 1975.

11. Foreman, pp. 54-58.

12. Sharp and Crofts, pp. 98-99.

13. Application of the president and directors of Georgetown College, Inc. 118 U.S. App. D.C. 80,331 F.2d 1000 (D.C. Cir. 1964).

14. Malone, pp. 306-310.

15. Black, Henry Campbell. *Black's law dictionary* (4th ed.). St. Paul, West Publishing Co., 1951. P. 488.

16. Sanger v. Butler. 101 S.W. 459 (1907).

17. Fitch v. Edwards. 239 Mo. App. 788 (1947).

18. Wassmer, Thomas A. Between life and death. Ethical and moral issues involved in recent medical advances. *Villanova Law Rev.* 13:772, 1968.

19. *Ibid.*, p. 773.

20. *Ibid.*, p. 774.

21. Olinger, Sheff D. Medical death. *Baylor Law Rev.* 27:25, 1975.

22. Conway, Daniel J. Medical and legal views of death: Confrontation and reconciliation *Saint Louis Law J.* 19:173, 1974.

23. Horan, Dennis J. Euthanasia, medical treatment and the mongoloid child: Death as a treatment of choice? *Baylor Law Rev.* 27:80, 1975.

24. Elkinton, J. Russel. The dying patient, the doctor, and the law. *Villanova Law Rev.* 13:747, 1968.

25. Report of the Commission on Medical Malpractice of the Secretary of Health, Education, and Welfare. Washington, D.C.: DHEW, January 16, 1973. P. 31.

26. Kansas Statutes Annotated. Sections 77-202 (Cum. Suppl. 1973).

27. California Health and Safety Code Section 7180 (West Suppl. 1974).

28. Conway, pp. 186-187.

29. Roth, Richard G. Legislation: The need for a current and effective statutory definition of death. *Oklahoma Law Rev.* 27:729, 1974.

30. State v. Brown. 8 Oreg. App. 72, 491 P.2d 1193 (1971).

31. Tucker v. Lower. No. 2831 (Richmond, Va., L. & Eq. Ct. filed May 23, 1972). (No appeal taken.)

32. In re Karen Quinlan. 69 N.J. 399 (1976).

12. WILLS AND
DECEDENTS' ESTATES

The power of an individual to make a legally binding disposition of his property on his death, although widely granted in most parts of the world, is neither universal nor uniform. Citizens of the United States enjoy in varying degrees a somewhat limited power to make this testamentary disposition by a will of the real estate and personal property they own at the time of their death. This right to make testamentary disposition of the property owned at death has its origin in primitive civilizations where it derived from ancestor worship and the desire for family continuity. In primitive societies, one without a descendant could appoint or nominate an heir. This was carried over into the Roman system and was more in the nature of an adoption than a testamentary disposition of property.

Under the Roman system, out of which evolved our present civil law, the power of a property owner to dispose of his property at the time of his death was restricted in order to protect his wife and children. Even today it may safely be said that there are greater restrictions on testamentary disposition to protect wives and children in civil-law jurisdictions than there are in those following the common law.

During the Roman occupation of Britain, the customs of Rome made a deep imprint on the British people and influenced the Anglo-Saxon society that followed. The advent of the feudal system of land tenure terminated the power to dispose of real estate by will in Great Britian. The practice of disposition of personal property by will continued and, after the Norman invasion, the use of wills gradually prevailed over the feudal system. By 1925, the last vestiges of the feudal system were removed from English law with the result that both real estate and personal property could be disposed of by will, subject to certain restrictions guarding the interest of wives and children.

The American colonies adopted in their charters the most liberal provisions of English laws pertaining to testamentary disposition (disposition by will). Certainly, since the Declaration of Independence citizens of the United States have had full power to make wills to dispose of real estate and personal property, subject to certain restrictions in favor of wives and children, which vary from state to state.

It should be pointed out, however, that the right to make a will and to dispose of one's property at death is neither a natural right nor a right guaranteed by the United States Constitution. Rather, it is a privilege granted by statute, without which a decedent's property would revert to the sovereign or to the state. For this reason, property disposed of by will may legally be subject to inheritance taxes. Generally, in the United States, a spouse cannot be completely disinherited by a will, but may elect to receive a share provided by statute. In the case of a widow, this share is called a dower right, and in the case of a widower, it is referred to as a right of courtesy. Furthermore, in most jurisdictions a child born after the execution of a will by its parent is not disinherited, but inherits as if the parent had died without a will.

Since the right to make a will is a mere statutory right, not a natural or constitutional right, the legislatures of the various states may prescribe the formalities required for the execution of a will. These formalities vary greatly from state to state. For example, New Jersey requires a "publication" by the person making the will, which is in fact a declaration that the instrument is a will, and further requires that the will be signed in the presence of two subscribing witnesses [1]. Pennsylvania, on the other hand, requires that a will be a writing showing dispositive intent, that is to say, showing the intent of the testator to dispose of his worldly goods at the time of his death. It must be signed at the end by the testator. There need be no subscribing witnesses in Pennsylvania, but two persons must swear that the signature at the end of the will is that of the testator [2].

PRACTICAL ASPECTS OF MAKING A WILL

What are some of the reasons that an apparently healthy young person, whether single or married, should go to a lawyer and pay a legal fee in order to have a will drawn?

1. First of all, wills are not the exclusive province of the aged and sick. Death may come without warning to any of us, especially the vast majority of us who travel on busy highways and fly from city to city. It is superfluous to point out that once a person is comatose or dead, it is too late to make a will. For those who die without a will, or *intestate*, the state will supply a will. Each state has a law providing for intestate distribution for its citizens who die without wills. Although the distribution may seem logical in the majority of cases, it certainly is not designed to fit the individual needs of everyone and it varies from state to state.

2. By means of a will a testator can not only provide for the manner in which his property is distributed at the time of his death, but also he can name a personal representative or executor of his choice to act for him after his death, to collect his assets, pay his debts and taxes, and make the distribution provided for in his will. If he has trust in this individual or institution, he can in his will waive a security bond, which is usually otherwise required by law, and thereby save his beneficiaries additional expense.

3. A will offers a testator who does not wish his beneficiaries to receive their gifts outright the opportunity to set up a testamentary trust, whereby

a designated individual or institution acts as trustee and holds the property for purposes and uses set forth in the will, such as providing income for an aged relative or funds for the education of a minor. The variations in trust arrangements are infinite and may be tailored to suit the wishes and needs of the person making a will.

In order to make the process of settling an estate more meaningful and easier to understand, it might be well to discuss the hypothetical case of a typical young family.

This family consisted of a father who was 40 years old, a wife 36, a daughter 12, and a son 7. The father had a middle-level executive job which, as a fringe benefit, provided him with $50,000 in life insurance, which he had made payable to his wife as primary beneficiary (if she did not survive him it would be payable to his children, share and share alike). In addition, he had approximately $20,000 in other life insurance policies with an identical designation of beneficiaries. The couple owned a house in which they had a $30,000 equity. Although the father earned what would generally be considered a good income, the family also had high expectations and maintained a high standard of living. He therefore had no will, having deferred the modest legal expense involved to other needs to which he had given a higher priority. Finally, a contemplated vacation involving an airplane flight as well as the death of a close friend without a will combined to persuade the head of this young family that the time had come for him to visit a lawyer.

The lawyer initially attempted to catalogue the family's assets. Although cash had never seemed plentiful, the husband was surprised to find that his estate would be worth in excess of $100,000. The lawyer pointed out to him that, although $100,000 might seem like an unimaginable sum to have in his possession during his lifetime, if he and his wife died the next day it would barely be adequate to provide maintenance and education for the two young children through college.

Since the family had set a college education as a minimum goal they wanted for their children, the lawyer recommended that the father purchase more life insurance, perhaps another $50,000 or $100,000 policy. He also pointed out that an equal distribution to the two children in the event that both parents died simultaneously would be unfair to the 7-year-old boy who had received five years less life support than his 12-year-old sister. Furthermore, the lawyer pointed out that the vicissitudes of life often make the needs of one child greater than those of another. If the parents were living they would certainly be willing to apply a greater part of their resources to help a sick child, and might want a similar flexibility in their estate. The lawyer suggested that in the event that the husband and wife died simultaneously the husband's assets, including his insurance, could be left to a trustee, preferably a bank, under a *sprinkle trust* arrangement whereby the bank would have the power to apply income and principal, if necessary, for the health, education, and welfare of the couple's children while they were under 21 years old. The bank would have no obligation to make equal application of the trust fund for the children prior to the time the younger child reached 21 years of age.

At such time as the couple had no living child under 21 years old, the trust would be terminated and the balance distributed equally to the children then living. Since they agreed on these general principles, the lawyer told the couple that he would prepare a draft of wills incorporating these provisions and others he thought advisable. He then proceeded to draft a will for the husband, providing for distribution of all of his assets outright to his wife if she survived him for 30 days, but otherwise to the trustee. The reason for the 30-day interval was the lawyer's desire to avoid burdening the couple's assets with double inheritance tax if the wife and the husband were injured in the same accident and the wife outlived the husband for a very short period of time. The couple named their bank as executor and trustee, giving it very broad discretionary powers regarding the manner in which the assets of their estates or trusts would be invested.

The lawyer in this case also inserted what is commonly known as a spendthrift clause. This provided that the assets of the estate or the trust would not be subject to the claims of creditors of the beneficiaries until actual distribution was made. The lawyer pointed out to the couple that they could name a guardian of the person for their children but that such a provision was not binding on the court since it is not possible to leave a human being to someone in the same manner that one can dispose of real estate or personal property. Such a provision providing a guardian of the person of minor children would be an expression of their wishes and be given some consideration by the court.

The lawyer suggested that a reciprocal will be prepared for the wife in the event that she survived the husband and received all of the assets of his estate.

After the wills were prepared and had been reviewed by the couple, they were executed in the presence of two subscribing witnesses. The lawyer suggested that the couple either leave the wills with him to be kept in his safe deposit box or place them in their own box. The husband had been somewhat reluctant to sign a will and had only done so as a result of the persistent urging of his wife, and because of the impending trip and the recent death of their friend. As the couple left, the lawyer assured them in a somewhat whimsical vein that the wills the couple had just signed were guaranteed not to shorten their lives by one second. Notwithstanding the assurance of the lawyer, the inevitable happened much sooner than anyone had expected. As a result of a mechanical defect, the airplane carrying the couple to their vacation crashed on takeoff and both were killed.

On being informed of the tragic news, the lawyer immediately consulted with the bank that had been appointed testamentary trustee and executor in the wills. The bank asked the lawyer to represent it and to file the wills for probate, whereupon the lawyer filed the wills with the court having jurisdiction over decedents' estates in the county in which the couple resided at the time of their deaths. He brought the two subscribing witnesses with him when he filed the wills in order that they might swear to the authenticity of the signatures of the testator and the testatrix. Once this was done and the necessary fees were paid, the court issued a certificate to the bank appointing it executor of the estates of the deceased couple. Such a certificate is commonly known as letters testamentary.

At this point the lawyer, acting on behalf of the bank, proceeded to gather the assets of the deceased couple's estate. He claimed whatever refunds were due on prepaid insurance policies, placed the house and automobiles for sale, and converted all the other assets to cash where it was practical to do so. He prepared and filed death tax returns for the state in which the couple resided and for the federal government. He established a bank account for the estate and deposited all cash assets of the estate into this account. Any of the decedents' outstanding debts were also paid.

Once the debts and taxes were paid and the assets were all collected and converted to cash if possible, the attorney prepared a final account for the bank. This account listed all the transactions that had taken place in the estates since the death of the decedents, and the assets, liabilities, and advance distributions, if any, made by the bank. The account was filed with the court along with a petition for a decree ordering distribution of the net assets of the estate to the trustee, to be applied according to the terms of the trust.

The court set a date for a public hearing, which is known as an audit, and of which all parties with an interest in the estates were required to be given notice. At the date of the audit, since no one appeared to object to the account and petition, the court ordered distribution made to the trustee as requested. The trustee, which was the same bank that had been executor, then held the net assets of the estate to be applied for the health, education, and welfare of the two children until they were both over twenty-one years old.

The provision in the will providing for guardian of the persons would never be considered by the court if the couple designated as guardians in the will took the children into their care when their parents died and nobody else wanted them. The only way in which the question of custody would come before the court would be in the event that there was a disagreement between two individuals or couples, each of whom wanted custody of the children. If one couple actually took them and the other couple instituted a legal action the matter would then come before the court. Of course, in the unlikely event that nobody came to claim the children, they would most likely end up in the hands of the local child welfare agency to be placed in a foster home.

There are certain terms that are commonly used by lawyers in connection with decedents' estates that it would be worthwhile for a layman to understand.

1. *A personal representative* is the individual or institution who, with authorization of the appropriate court, acts for a person after he dies to collect his assets, pay his debts, and make distribution of his estate in accordance with his will or in accordance with the applicable intestate law, if the decedent died without a will. A personal representative appointed in a will is known as an executor, or in the case of a woman, an executrix. If the personal representative has not been named in a will, he or it is known as an administrator, and if a female, as an administratrix.

2. Bequests are frequently made to an issue or class of people *per stirpes*. The easiest way to explain this would be by example. If a testator

left his entire estate to his issue per stirpes and left one child and the two children of another deceased child surviving him, then his two grand-children would each get one-quarter and his surviving child would get one-half of his estate. Per stirpes distribution is also referred to as distribution by representation.

DEATH TAXES

When an individual dies his assets are subject to two types of death tax. State death taxes, generally referred to as inheritance taxes, are usually at a flat rate and are generally imposed on assets that were in the possession of the decedent at the time of his death and on insurance policies and other interests that are payable to the estate of the decedent and therefore pass through the hands of the executor or the administrator. Generally, property held as tenants by the entireties (jointly with a spouse) is not subject to state inheritance tax. Property held jointly with another not the spouse may be subject to state inheritance tax to the extent of the decedent's interest in such property.

Death taxes imposed by the federal government generally attach to more property than those imposed by the individual states. For instance, a decedent's taxable estate for purposes of the federal estate tax includes many items or interests passing as a result of the decedent's death that would not in most jurisdictions be subject to state death taxes. The aggregate of the interests that are subject to federal estate taxes are referred to as the decedent's gross estate, and when a deducation is made for the expenses of administration it is referred to as the adjusted gross estate. In addition to assets normally subject to state death taxes, the adjusted gross estate generally includes all property interests owned by the decedent at the time of his death, to the extent of the value of such interests. For instance, a piece of real estate owned by the decedent and his spouse would be included, as would insurance policies on decedent's life which were owned by decedent and payable to his wife rather than his estate.

The federal estate tax, unlike most state inheritance taxes, is a graduated tax whereby smaller estates are taxed at a lower rate than larger ones.

A detailed discussion of the Tax Reform Act of 1976 is beyond the scope of this text. However, certain general observations may be made. This important piece of federal legislation has given each decedent a unified tax credit against federal estate and gift taxes. This credit increases in annual steps during the phase-in period of the Act to $47,000 for decedents dying in 1981 or thereafter.

Although prior to the 1976 Act, a federal estate tax return was required for any decedent who had a gross estate in excess of $60,000, under the new law this threshold is raised in annual steps during the phase-in period of the Act so that for decedents dying on or after January 1, 1981, a federal estate tax return need only be filed if the gross estate is in excess of $175,000.

In the case of decedents who are married at the time of their death, another deduction is available. As a general rule, subject to certain exceptions, the decedent can leave up to 50 percent of the property constituting his adjusted gross estate or $250,000, whichever is greater to a surviving spouse, free and clear of federal estate taxes. This is known as the marital deduction. Perhaps this concept may be clarified by an example. Assume, for example, that Mr. A. died in 1981 leaving a will making his wife his sole beneficiary, and his entire adjusted gross estate in the amount of $800,000 passed to his wife as a result of his death. Of the $800,000, one-half, or $400,000 would not be subject to federal estate tax by virtue of the marital deduction. A tax credit of $47,000 would be allowed against the estate tax otherwise due on the remaining $400,000, subject to certain adjustments for gifts made during the decedent's lifetime.

ANATOMICAL GIFTS

Recent advances in medical science have greatly increased the use of body parts taken from cadavers in restoring function to the bodies of living individuals. With new progress constantly being made to overcome tissue rejection, cases of organ and tissue transplant are proliferating.

Medical schools and other institutions that train individuals preparing for careers in the health care field are constantly looking for cadavers to satisfy the needs of the human anatomy classes. Unclaimed bodies in prisons, poorhouses, and elsewhere are insufficient to satisfy the needs for dissection and research, and for body parts for transplantation. In response to these needs, many enlightened individuals have asked that on their death their bodies be utilized for some worthwhile purpose, whether for donation to a medical school for instructional purposes or for use in transplant procedures.

Forty-nine states have adopted, in one form or another, the Uniform Anatomical Gift Act, which sets standards by which a dead body may be utilized for these worthwhile purposes [3]. The Act provides that any person who has attained his majority may give all or any part of his body for research, transplantation, education, or for the general advancement of medical science, and may designate as the donee any hospital, surgeon, physician, medical or dental school, or anatomical board.

An anatomical gift under the Act is invalid unless made in writing at least fifteen days prior to the donor's death. After the death of the donor, if he has expressed no intent to the contrary, his next of kin, with first priority being given to the surviving spouse, may donate the decedent's body or any part thereof to the same donees and for the same purposes. The Anatomical Gift Act sets a priority among the next of kin with the surviving spouse having first priority and adult children having the next priority proceeding downward through parents and adult brothers and sisters.

In the absence of a specified donee and any expressed indication of contrary intent on the part of the donor, the attending physician may accept an anatomical gift as donee. This is so whether the donor fails to designate the donee or whether the donee is not available.

An anatomical gift may be made by signing a document, which need not be a will but which may be a simple donor card kept in a place which indicates the donor's intention that it be valid. It need not be delivered to the specified donee but may be kept in a bank vault, storage facility, registry office, or on the donor's person until his death.

If, in fact, the document has been delivered to the donee, the donor may amend or revoke the gift by delivering a signed written statement of his intentions to the donee, by making an oral declaration of his intention to revoke the gift in the presence of two persons and communicating it to the donee, by telling the physician attending him during a terminal illness or injury that he intends to amend or revoke the gift, which statement must be communicated to the donee, or by keeping on his person or among his effects a signed writing declaring his intention to amend or revoke the gift.

Of course, the signed document indicating an intention to make an anatomical gift that has not been delivered to the donee may be revoked by the donor by any of the preceeding methods or by simply destroying it or mutilating it in some manner that indicates his intention to revoke it.

Under the Anatomical Gift Act, there is no obligation on the part of the donee to accept an anatomical gift. Furthermore, there is a provision in the Act that protects any person attempting to comply with the provisions of the Act in good faith from being subject to criminal prosecution or liability as a result of a civil action for damages.

AUTOPSY

In general, postmortem examinations of the deceased by a licensed physician or osteopath may be authorized in writing by the deceased during his lifetime or in writing by his surviving spouse after the deceased's death. In the absence of a surviving spouse, most states allow the next of kin, in a prescribed order of priority, to give such authorization. Generally, however, such authorization may only be given by the next of kin who claims the body for burial.

Under the laws of most states, a dead body remaining unclaimed for burial for a specified period of time falls under the jurisdiction of the state's anatomical board and may be used for any authorized purpose for which a donor could donate his body [4].

CONTRACTS WITH DECEDENTS

Contracts with the decedent that involve personal service may be terminated when it was the personal qualities of the decedent that were the inducement to the contract. For instance, the death of a nurse who was under contract to perform private nursing services to an individual patient for an extended period of time would not obligate her estate to supply another nurse to complete the contract.

UNDUE INFLUENCE

Periodically, human interest stories appear in the newspapers involving an elderly decedent who left his or her entire estate to a companion or nurse. Frequently a bitter will contest is involved, with the next of kin of the deceased person alleging undue influence on the part of the nurse or companion. While such cases are relatively uncommon, they are very dramatic and often receive a great deal of publicity. Undue influence, if proved, is a ground for setting aside a will. It exists when the relationship between two people is such that one is unable to exercise his free will and, by virtue of such lack of free will, is influenced to make provisions in his will that he would not have otherwise made. Such undue influence may exist because of a confidential relationship between the parties, as in the case of an attorney and client, or because of weakness and impairment of intellect on the part of the testator. Children may exercise undue influence on a weak and mentally impaired parent, and nurses may, under some circumstances, exercise such undue influence on a weak, dependent, and mentally impaired patient.

Wills procured by such means may be set aside; however, the burden of proving such undue influence generally rests on the parties attacking the will. In some jurisdictions, if a person is in a confidential relationship to the decedent, such as a nurse taking care of an aged and infirm patient, and that nurse procures a lawyer to write a will in which the nurse is named as a beneficiary by the decedent, then the burden of proof shifts to the nurse to disprove undue influence.

In many cases nurses are asked to witness wills. It is a nurse's privilege to decline such a request, especially if she believes that the patient is not in command of his or her mental faculties and is unable to exercise free will. If she does witness the signature of a patient, she may be called on to attest to its validity if the patient dies and the will is probated. While it is certainly a moral duty to aid a dying person who wishes to make a will, it would also seem prudent for a nurse to decline to act as a witness in cases in which the will is being executed by someone whose mental capacity or independence she has reason to doubt.

It might also be added that the mere existence of a nurse-patient relationship does not of itself establish undue influence. A patient in full control of his mental faculties may certainly make the nurse or companion taking care of him the beneficiary of his estate, no matter what its size. The will is set aside only if a person standing in a confidential relationship to the deceased actually and effectively exercised undue influence on the deceased in such a way that the deceased was deprived of his or her free will, and executed the will by reason of such undue influence.

REFERENCES

1. New Jersey Statutes Annotated, Title 3A, Section 3-2.
2. Pennsylvania Consolidated Statutes Annotated, Title 20, Sections 2502 and 3132.
3. Uniform Anatomical Gift Act, Chicago, National Conference of Commissioners on Uniform State Laws, 1968.
4. Jackson, Percival E. *The law of cadavers and burial places* (2nd ed.). New York: Prentice Hall, Inc., 1950. P. 166.

13. PRINCIPLES FOR NURSES TO REMEMBER

Do you swear to tell the truth, the whole
truth, and nothing but the truth
so help you God?

There you sit with your hand on the Bible saying "I do" as you are sworn in as a witness before the jury. Until you received the suit papers or the subpoena that has brought you to court, you might have forgotten even caring for this patient, who is now the plaintiff responsible for your presence on the witness stand.

A patient or family sues for acts or omissions, either imagined or real, when there has been no rapport built between the nursing staff and the patient and his family. Nursing is a helping profession that is oriented toward service to fellow human beings who naturally do not want to be treated cruelly in an efficient, stuffy manner. Rather, they want to be treated by a nurse knowledgeable in her field who expresses warmth and concern for their health and their dignity. Besides the nursing care itself, the most important factor in malpractice suits is the nurse-patient relationship. This has been found to be true so often that health institutions are setting up inservice programs on human relations in a defensive effort to lessen malpractice suits.

It will be much easier for you to relax on the witness stand if you have protection for yourself against negligence suits in the form of nurse's professional liability insurance. The suit-consciousness of the public has resulted in an increased number of claims being filed against health professionals. A professional nurse is accountable for the welfare of the patient. Nurses are liable for negligence that causes injury to another person or to his possessions. Professional liability insurance can remedy the great weight placed on professionals not only by providing protection from money damages, but also by paying the legal expenses incurred to defend any claims or suits brought, whether meritorious or not.

When a negligence suit is filed and the suit papers are served on a nurse, in our legal system the nurse is required to defend herself. If a nurse fails to defend herself, she is presumed liable. For a nurse, not to be covered by professional liability insurance means to assume a grave financial risk. The uninsured professional nurse is legally liable to pay damages herself for the results of her negligence. If she failed to defend herself or lost a negligence suit, she would have to pay both the legal expense, if any, and the judgment for money damages. Depending on the amount of the

153

judgment, the nurse could lose her savings account, her car, and even her home.

Malpractice or professional liability insurance for nurses who are not nurse anesthetists remains very reasonable today. Policies with high limits are available at a modest cost. A sample of a typical professional liability policy for nurses is given in Appendix II.

Most professional liability insurance policies for nurses are written on an "occurrence" basis. This means that the policyholder is protected against claims for occurrences during the policy period, even though the claims are made after the policy has expired, up to periods that vary according to the jurisdiction and the particular policy. Such coverage is important to nurses, for claims against them may be made years after an occurrence. For example, in many jurisdictions the statute of limitations does not start to run on a claim for an injury until it is or should have been discovered. Therefore, claims for a sponge or an instrument left in a patient's body could be made years after an operation, so long as suit was filed within the statutory period after the condition was discovered.

With the increase in malpractice claims against nurses and physicians in recent years, insurance companies have been seeking ways to limit their liability. Some insurance companies are now writing "claims only" policies, which limit coverage to claims made during the policy period. Such policies may cost less than occurrence policies, but the disadvantage to the policyholder is obvious. Under the provisions of a claims only policy, a nurse who leaves the practice of nursing and drops her professional liability insurance will have no coverage for a later claim for an incident occurring during the policy period. In short, the occurrence policies cost more, but offer a nurse much better protection.

As with most liability insurance, the initial coverage is the most expensive, and to increase the limits up to $1 million is not costly compared with the original premium. The high rate of inflation has affected court verdicts. Today, it is not unusual for $500,000 and more (sometimes in excess of $1 million) to be awarded in a death case. What a horrendous experience it would be to discover that the limit of your professional liability insurance was $100,000 less than the amount specified in the jury's verdict. Having adequate malpractice insurance can save the nurse the worry and expense of vindicating herself and allow her to expend her energies on providing quality nursing care rather than worrying about legal liability.

Nurses need to realize that, although they may maintain "perfect" nursing performance, they can be sued. Once having been sued, they must defend themselves. It is not an unusual approach for a lawyer to acquire the records from a health institution in which his client claims to have received negligent care and to sue everyone whose name appears on those records. This is referred to as the shotgun approach, and its purpose is to have a great number of insurance companies involved in the settlement of the case. With several insurance companies contributing to the kitty, it does not take a legal genius to know that more money will be available for a settlement than if only one company is involved.

In the past, malpractice suits involving nurses were generally filed against an institution or a physician as employer or superior. It was thought that nurses made little money, had few possessions, and generally did not carry insurance. Today all this has changed; nurses now have higher salaries and more possessions, and a great number carry malpractice insurance. For this reason, the nurse who fails to carry professional liability insurance does so at her own risk.

Nursing has a good public image. Juries tend to react favorably toward nurses and to believe what they say. In a courtroom situation there is not time to live down the image that a first impression makes. Therefore, it behooves a nurse appearing in court to be aware of her appearance. Whereas a juror ought to judge objectively the evidence before him, to deny that jurors are influenced by subjective impressions of how one looks, one's personality, and one's speech would not be giving a true picture. One should dress attractively, attempting to look as the general public presumes professionals should; this would mean not dressing in any extreme.

Prior to testifying, the nurse should review her knowledge of the scope of nursing today, the nurse practice act of the state in which she works, and the agency policies of the institution in which she was working at the time the care under question was given. Being on the witness stand is an emotionally tiring and uncomfortable situation, as is sitting in the courtroom and listening to others testify either for or against you. This uncomfortable situation is better dealt with when the patient's chart and, more particularly, the nurse's notes reflect an honest, factual, and well-written record of the patient's stay in the health institution. The nurse is responsible for providing quality care to the patient and good service to her employing agency. She should not attempt to protect her employer by covering her own or others' errors. The nurse is truly accountable when the patient's chart reflects objective recording of the nursing problems assessed and the solutions applied. Vital information which was not assessed at the proper time should not be squeezed between the lines on a patient's record.

If a negligent act is committed, it should be charted along with the measures taken to correct the situation. Nurses are human beings, and as such are capable of committing errors and omissions. An incident report should be completed for the health institution. This should be noted on the patient's record and the institution should be put on notice that the incident is to be reported to its insurance company. If the negligent act discovered on the record was committed by the nurse herself, rather than by someone else and then discovered by her, the nurse should inform her malpractice insurance company.

Many practicing registered nurses have told us of pressures put on them by health institutions to rewrite nurses' notes after the patient has been discharged and there is an indication that suit is going to be brought by the patient or his family. This is a most unprofessional request that questions the moral values of the nurse involved. If you are sitting in the witness chair at this point and are being asked if in fact this chart reveals the actual care received by the patient, you have placed yourself in a very serious position. To commit perjury is a felony and something we are sure that nurses never intend to commit. In addition, in a malpractice suit in which there are many defendants, the nurse might find herself in a position where an attorney for her employer might attempt to prove that she did something that the health institution itself forbids. Then the employer's attorney and the plaintiff's attorney might join forces in attempting to prove the nurse guilty of malpractice. Honesty is the best policy in our professional as well as in our private lives.

PATIENT AUDITS

In 1970, the Joint Commission of Accreditation of Hospitals changed their standards of care from only requiring hospitals to provide the minimum or essential patient care, to requiring hospitals to strive for optimum patient care. The Commission believes that today health care delivery is a shared responsibility and that audits evaluating care need to be patient audits rather than medical audits alone [1]. The issue need not be who is providing the care, but whether the care is being provided. The health professions appear to be moving toward an integrated patient audit which will reveal those areas of patient care that need procedural or policy changes. Patient audits should indicate whether a nurse's performance needs further evaluation. This appears to us to be a desirable means of providing professional accountability in health-related fields. It presumes a knowledge on the part of the professions of the services each profession has to offer. Most professional groups like to present a unified position to the public and hesitate to evaluate their professional peers. Nurses must be careful not to follow the example of some physicians in their legal accountability by being unwilling to testify in a courtroom setting as to what constitutes reasonable nursing care. The trust placed in the nursing profession by the health care consumer must be acknowledged by adequate policing of the nursing profession by nurses themselves.

Patient care audits are certainly a necessity, but so are evaluations of nursing practice by nursing administrators. A nurse's performance should be evaluated at least annually, and preferably semiannually. Evaluation forms should be developed to evaluate the competencies required for nursing performance of good quality within a particular institution. Once the evaluation is developed, it is important to decide what minimum standards need to be met in order for employment to be continued and what resources are available within the institution to provide for the growth or the remedial needs of those employed. This type of honest appraisal of nurses will provide the feedback needed by the employed professional, and will protect the consumer.

Increased interdependence of health care professionals has mandated a new need for understanding, cooperation, and communication among all of the health care providers. That providers are talking about a patient audit means that the focus is now on patient care rather than on traditional medical care, nursing care, physical therapy, and the like.

RECORD KEEPING

One means of turning the ideal of good patient care into a reality is abandoning the traditional practice of having separate records for the physician, nurse, and therapist. The new problem-oriented record approach to patient care puts the emphasis on the patient and his problems. This is in contrast to the source-oriented record where entries are filed on the chart according to what source they come from, for example, nurses' notes, physicians' notes, laboratory reports, and physical therapy reports. The problem-oriented record is an integrated record of the patient's problems. The four basic components of the problem-oriented record are: data base, problem list, plan, and notes [2].

The data base is the routine or standard information that needs to be known about any individual in a particular health care setting. The general history, physical examination, physiologic and laboratory data, as well as the nurse's history regarding the patient's current status and life-style, are all part of the data base. There should be only one data base section for any patient's active record. This provides a meaningful resource containing information from a variety of sources.

The problem list includes aspects of the patient's health that require intervention because they may produce or threaten to produce disability, morbidity, or an increased risk of mortality. Each problem requires a plan. Physicians and nurses complement each other in a unified effort to propose a plan of care for a patient. The plan should include specific doctor and nurse activity as well as patient-oriented objectives. The patient care plan should (1) meet the physical care and other needs of the patient, (2) provide a teaching plan for the patient to understand both his treatment and his illness, and (3) include a discharge plan providing for continuity of care in cases in which this is needed.

The problem-oriented approach requires a single section for progress notes in which all those participating in the patient's care can document their findings, assessment, plans, and orders. The progress notes should be written following a mental process similar to one that has been described frequently as SOAP, which is an acronym for subjective data, objective data, assessment, and plan [3].

Subjective data include all information which can be obtained by speaking with the patient. Objective data come from observing the patient, physical examination, laboratory findings, x-rays, and other tests. Assessment refers to the analysis of both the subjective and the objective data and their interrelationship with the patient's various problems. Plan refers here to the adaptation of the original patient care plan component of the problem-oriented record. It is not essential to include each entry within the SOAP recording method each time a note is written. The SOAP plan is a mental process much like the nursing process itself. Implementation and evaluation are essential parts of this conceptual framework and there is inherent in the process much critical thought. The problem-oriented record should eliminate duplication and extraneous material from the record and provide a concise, clear picture of the patient. An important part of the progress notes is the use of appropriate flow sheets whereby routine observations can be recorded providing for good quality control and easy retrievability for patient audits.

As in all records, a judge or jury may assume a nurse to be careless if she writes on the chart in a careless manner and with numerous spelling and punctuation errors. It is important for all who read the record to derive the meaning that was intended. We wish to borrow an example used by Alice Kerr in her article "Nurses' Notes," in which she demonstrates how a statement can be interpreted according to one's own personal bias. An English teacher gave a college class this sentence to punctuate: "Woman without her man is nothing." The men wrote, "Woman, without her man, is nothing," and the women wrote, "Woman, without her, man is nothing" [4].

A nurse is to report her observations in a factual manner, avoiding the use of the statement "It appears to be," and giving opinions that are only useful if one knows the point of reference from which they are made. A correct, accurate record of the care the patient received in a health institution is the best documentation of good health care. An analogy can be made between winning a football game and coming up smelling like a rose in a malpractice suit in court. A good offense—a well-documented, problem-oriented record—is the best defense.

The recent growth in consumerism has brought a new concern over who can have access to health institution records and to whom these records belong. In the absence of special provisions, the health records are generally considered to be the property of the health institution, physician, or nurse practitioner since it is necessary for proper administration to maintain these records. However, just as one's right to own a firearm does not give one the right to use it to unlawfully kill another person, a health institution's ownership of the record does not give it the right to violate the patient's or client's privacy. There is a dearth of case law in this area; however, we feel an analogy can be drawn from the recent decisions regarding the student's right of access to his academic records, which remain the property of the educational institution. We think that future case law will support the premise that the patient has the right of access to his own medical or health records. It is generally accepted that patients do have the right to confidentiality in regard to the records of their health history and treatment. This is why patients are asked to sign a form giving the treating person or agency permission to release confidential and personal health information to another health care professional, health care institution, or an agency or person outside the health care field before this information is shared. It is a general principle of law that when a plaintiff sues for professional malpractice he waives the need for consent or voluntary disclosure, allowing the defendant access to the health records if he himself happens not to be the owner of the record.

The foregoing includes our opinion of what the future holds in store, but we would be remiss if we did not relate that currently, in many jurisdictions, the health institution or physician may refuse to disclose health records to the patient or to his legal representative in the absence of a legal proceeding.

It is universally accepted in the United States that a medical consent must be based on adequate information in order to be valid. During the admission procedure in most health institutions a patient is asked to sign a general, or so-called blanket, form of consent for the treatment expected. The patient may be asked at a later date to sign consent for specific diagnostic tests or for surgical procedures.

At present there are two definitions of what informed consent actually includes [5]. The majority opinion holds that in order for an individual to give informed consent, he must receive an explanation by the physician that contains the details generally supplied in similar circumstances by the medical profession of that locale. In jurisdictions following the majority rule, a plaintiff wishing to prove lack of informed consent must produce an expert witness offering testimony on what information is generally given by the medical profession in that geographic area.

Jurisdictions that follow the minority opinion have eliminated a need for expert testimony by ruling that the amount of information required prior to receiving informed consent is that which a reasonable man would need to know in order to make an intelligent decision. With the current

interest in patient's rights, it appears that the blanket consent form has little legal value and that more jurisdictions will eventually follow what is today the minority rule on consent.
consent.

A nurse must realize that there is a need for medical disclosure regarding the choices of treatment for a particular individual. Although nurses are frequently asked to fill in the consent form and witness the signature, they are not responsible for the explanation of medical care to the patient as it relates to informed consent. The nurse is merely witnessing the patient's signature, an act that could be done by any layman. The nurse should be alert to the fact that in this highly educated country there remain many who lack literacy and who cover up their inadequacy quite well. A nurse does have an obligation to inform a physician that a patient is unable to read the consent form. It is important to realize that when a patient signs a consent form he has not given up the right to change his mind; he can do this verbally at any time prior to treatment. It is certainly a nurse's responsibility to bring this change of mind to the physician's attention and not to aid in giving care to a patient who she knows wishes to refuse such treatment.

In witnessing the signature on a consent form the nurse should be aware that an individual giving consent should be fully in control of his faculties. If a patient cannot sign his name, an "X" is an acceptable signature when it is written in a manner prescribed within the jurisdiction. For example, one jurisdiction requires the "X" to be written in the middle of the patient's name. The witness would write "Mary ____ Smith." Over the blank, she would inscribe "her" and below the blank, "mark." Mary Smith would then mark her "X" in that blank space. Two individuals are then required to witness the "X" signature as belonging to Mary Smith.

In the nurse practice acts, nurses have been charged with providing patient education as part of nursing care. It is now both a legal and an ethical obligation to explain nursing care and to teach personal health care.

As nurse clinics are expanding to provide health care more economically to more citizens, nurses need to be aware that many jurisdictions provide that no consent for nursing care is needed in a true emergency; that is, when delaying treatment would jeopardize the life of the patient.

Most jurisdictions provide that minors within their jurisdictions can be treated in an emergency without parental or guardian consent. If it is not an emergency and the minor is not emancipated, then the institution should petition the court to appoint a guardian. If a physician or other health provider treats a minor without parental or guardian consent inadvertently, relying in good faith on the representation of the minor, he is in some jurisdictions not liable for rendering service. In most cases appealed to the courts in which parents have refused treatment that medical authorities felt would prolong the life of a child, the court has permitted the treatment, for example, blood transfusion. Some jurisdictions also provide for the diagnosis and treatment of venereal disease and pregnancy without parental consent.

It is of the utmost importance to the nursing profession today for all nurses to be aware of the scope of nursing. Nurses need to be aware of their legal responsibilities and moral obligations. Physicians cannot take responsibility for what nurses do. If nurses are to achieve equal status with the medical profession and other health professionals, they must stand up for their rights. A nurse who is not an advocate for nursing is not an advocate for her patients either. It is irresponsible for nurses to take on themselves responsibility that is not within their legal scope. Performing a medical procedure because the nurse does not wish to awaken a physician in the middle of the night, working a double shift, and taking charge in a coronary care unit for which she has not been trained are acts of unprofessional conduct equal in culpability to any omission of nursing care.

This above all: to thine own self be true,
And it must follow, as the night the day,
Thou canst not then be false to any man [6].

To paraphrase Shakespeare in *Hamlet*, a nurse who is true to professional ideals will not betray the trust of the patient.

REFERENCES
1. American Hospital Association. *Quality assurance program for medical care in the hospital.* Chicago, Illinois, 1972.
2. Yarnall, Steven R., and Atwood, Judith. Problem-oriented practice for nurses and physicians. *Nurs. Clin.* 9:218, 1974.
3. McCloskey, Joanne Comi. The problem-oriented record vs. the nursing care plan: A proposal. *Nurs. Outlook* 23:492, 1975.
4. Kerr, Alice H. Nursing notes. *Nursing '75* 5:41, 1975.
5. Irene Cooper, Appellant v. Dr. Brooke Roberts; Irene Cooper, Appellant v. Dr. Norman Nathan Cohen. 220 Pennsylvania Superior Court 260, 286 A2d 647 (1971).
6. Shakespeare, William. *Hamlet*, Act I, scene 3.

APPENDIX I. AMERICAN NURSES' ASSOCIATION GUIDELINES FOR THE INDIVIDUAL NURSE CONTRACT

AMERICAN NURSES' ASSOCIATION

GUIDELINES FOR THE INDIVIDUAL NURSE CONTRACT

The following pages incorporate proposals and comments concerning the individual nurse contract. It is probable that changes and additions based on the particular employment situation will be desirable in order to obtain the most advantageous provisions under the circumstances. The nurse can delete those sections which she does not wish to utilize.

The nurse ordinarily negotiates her own contract with the employer, but she may wish to consult the State Economic and General Welfare Personnel in the Association Office.

An alternative to bargaining for time off covering vacation, sick leave, holidays, and educational leave would be an all inclusive 60 paid working days per year for the nurse to use at her own discretion. None of the above will then have to be listed specifically.

Do not be disappointed if your first venture into establishing a written contract results in less than you would desire as an ultimate. Bargaining or negotiating means a give and take between parties. Do remember that each time you renegotiate you will make strides and you will gain additional benefits each and every year. In the form of a written contract the gains are made stable and more easily administered.

SUGGESTED CONTRACT LANGUAGE	BASIS FOR JUSTIFICATION

This agreement is entered into this _____ day of _____ by and between the _____ (hospital, clinic or individual physician) hereinafter referred to as the employer and (name of individual nurse) hereinafter referred to as the employee.

Witnesseth:
Whereas it is the desire of the parties to this Agreement to promote mutual cooperation and understanding in the interest of maintaining quality patient care and to formulate rules to govern the relationship between them, now therefore, the parties agree as follows:

SUGGESTED CONTRACT LANGUAGE	BASIS FOR JUSTIFICATION	NOTATIONS

ARTICLE I
Duties, Responsibilities and Authority

The duties, responsibility and authority of the nurse position shall be as follows: _____

Include job title, job description and lines of authority.

ARTICLE II
Salary

The employer will pay _____ salary per month or _____ per year.

In some work settings a probationary period may be required and the salary is less during this period. The probationary period would be negotiable unless within a civil service structure.

A yearly increase (increment) should be negotiated with payment started automatically on the anniversary date of employment each year. This would be over and above the cost of living increase negotiable when the contract is reopened.

ARTICLE III
Hours of Work and Premium Pay

Proposal #1: Time and one-half shall be paid for all work in excess of 8 hours per day or 40 hours per week.

Proposal #1: The negotiated salary is usually based upon a 40 hour work week. It is contemplated that nurses will frequently work additional hours.

If contemplating innumerable hours of overtime and taking calls (nurse practitioners, etc.) negotiate a more substantial salary in lieu of all overtime and special on-call benefits.

SUGGESTED CONTRACT LANGUAGE	BASIS FOR JUSTIFICATION	NOTATIONS
ARTICLE IV Vacation Vacation with pay will be at the rate of ____ working days per month and cumulative up to ____ working days. Vacations will be scheduled only after consultation with and approval of the employee.	The goal would be to negotiate one months vacation per year not including holidays.	
ARTICLE V Holidays Holidays with pay will include the following: 1. 2. 3. 4. 5. 6. 7. 8. 9. 10. 11. 12.	The number of holidays vary usually from 8 to 12. Some contracts now specify the employee's birthday. If the employee has elected Proposal #1 under Article III -- overtime for holidays should be negotiated. Nurses in some instances are realizing double pay for holidays. If the employee negotiates under Proposal #2, Article III, she must be aware of the trends established in receiving more pay for holiday time.	
ARTICLE VI Nursing Education The parties recognize the need for the employee to participate in continuing education programs. The term education or educational as used in this article shall include, but not be limited to, workshops, seminars, conferences, clinics and other professional activities.	Depending upon the circumstances a specific number of days for educational leave may be negotiated per year. If flexibility is desired, use the articles without including a specific number of days.	

SUGGESTED CONTRACT LANGUAGE	BASIS FOR JUSTIFICATION	NOTATIONS

Article VI - Nursing Education (continued)

Any educational program required by the employer will be funded by the employer.

The employee may request attendance in an educational program or course of instruction and the employer will approve such request if the following conditions are met:

   a. The educational program or course of instruction is related to the employee's job and will improve the professional skills to meet the needs of the employee.

   b. Attendance in the educational program or course of instruction will not unreasonably disrupt the normal operations of the employer.

ARTICLE VII
Sabbatical Leave

The employer will grant sabbatical leave to the employee after seven years service with the employer as a registered professional nurse. Such leave shall not extend beyond one year.

In reviewing a request for sabbatical leave the employer will consider and may approve on the following basis:

   a. The nature and length of professional educational course work, research or other professional activity which the employee plans to undertake during the sabbatical leave.

To tighten the effectiveness of educational leave the following addition may be made:

"In the event the employer is unable in good faith to grant the educational leave request the employer will set forth in writing the reasons for the denial."

   b. May be used as an excuse by the employer, but conversely may make the article more acceptable.

For your information there is a precedent established for sabbatical leave in a group contract covering 620 nurses in Hawaii.

All university contracts should cover sabbatical as well.

SUGGESTED CONTRACT LANGUAGE	BASIS FOR JUSTIFICATION	NOTATIONS
Article VII - Sabbatical Leave (continued) b. Whether the employee's absence during the leave will adversely affect providing essential services. Employee while on sabbatical leave will paid an amount equal to one-half of the compensation which the employee was receiving at commencement of leave. The payments shall be made in regular monthly installments. Prior to the start of a sabbatical leave the employee and employer will enter into a supplement to this agreement which shall provide for the following: a. The employee will agree to return to work upon expiration of the sabbatical leave. b. Upon return from the sabbatical leave the employee will agree to work in the appropriate department for a period of two continuous years. c. The employee will be guaranteed return to the same or equivalent position at the expiration of the sabbatical leave. d. Upon the employee's return the salary rate will be the same as at the time of leave and the increment date will be advanced equivalent to the duration of the leave. The employee will not be deprived of any accumulated vacation allowance or sick leave credit but shall not accrue vacation allowance or sick leave	b. Is again debatable but may be necessary. d. Salary upon return is negotiable but should never be less than when sabbatical started.	

SUGGESTED CONTRACT LANGUAGE	BASIS FOR JUSTIFICATION	NOTATIONS
ARTICLE VIII Other Benefits The employee shall be eligible to participate in the following employee benefit plans: 1. 2. 3.	A reminder to check other benefit plans and include a clause in the contract. As a substitute a clause may be used stating "This agreement shall not be construed or applied in any manner to impair or diminish any existing rights, privileges or benefits which would otherwise be available to the employee."	
ARTICLE IX Sick Leave The employee will be entitled to sick leave with pay on the basis of _____ working days for each month of continuous employment cumulative to _____ working days. Sick leave will be allowed for medical, dental, optical and optometrical appointments which cannot be scheduled during off-duty time.	Sick leave is usually accrued at one day per month. The accumulation of leave varies greatly. An accumulation of several months becomes valuable. Sick leave can now be used for maternity leave. Maternity leave has not been discussed as the woman's equal rights under EEOC Guidelines delineate she use maternity leave at her own discretion with consultation from her personal physician. The employee's return to her position is guaranteed. Employers can no longer establish regulations discriminatory against the pregnant woman.	

SUGGESTED CONTRACT LANGUAGE	BASIS FOR JUSTIFICATION	NOTATIONS
ARTICLE X Leave of Absence for Death in the Family The employee will be allowed three working days as funeral leave with pay which will not be deducted from any other leave to which the employee may be entitled. Funeral leaves will be granted on such days as designated by the employee provided they fall within a reasonable period of time after a death in the immediate family. ARTICLE XI Health Benefits	The meaning of family is a negotiable item. Alternative or in addition to would be an article titled Personal Leave. The employee could use ___ days per year at their own discretion for personal business. Existing medical coverage plans vary to an unbelieveable degree. In state, city and county employment nurses are usually covered by the civil service benefits applied to all employees in that system. The applicant must investigate what exists and if the programs are inadequate, must negotiate for individual coverage. Retirement plans also vary. In many instances, in the private sector you must be employed for 2 years before being eligible to participate with little or no vesting for 5 to 15 years. Many nurses match employer's funds monthly for a better retirement program.	

SUGGESTED CONTRACT LANGUAGE	BASIS FOR JUSTIFICATION	NOTATIONS

ARTICLE XII
Transportation

Mileage for the use of personal automobiles will be computed from the employee's first call or from his official work station to his return to that station.

Mileage runs 10-12¢ per mile ordinarily. There are existing contracts that cover a car allowance if the car is used daily and heavily. This allowance in some instances is $50 per month.

IRS allows 12¢ per mile. If the full 12¢ cannot be negotiated, the remainder can be claimed as an income tax deduction if records are adequate.

ARTICLE XIII
The Grievance Procedure

It is the intention of the parties that an employee grievance which arises out of alleged violation, misinterpretation or misapplication of this agreement shall be resolved in accordance with provisions set forth herein.

In state civil service a grievance procedure probably already exists.

Definition of a grievance: The term "grievance" as used in this agreement shall mean a complaint filed by the employee alleging a violation, misinterpretation or misapplication of a specific provision of this agreement occuring after its effective date. A grievance shall, whenever possible, be discussed and settled informally between the employee and their immediate supervisor. The employee may, if they desire, be assisted by a representative of their Nurses' Association.

Article XIII - The Grievance Procedure (continued)

Formal steps:

Step 1: If the matter is not satisfactorily settled on an informal basis, the employee
may institute a formal grievance by
setting forth in writing the nature
of the complaint, the specific term or
provision of the agreement allegedly
violated and the remedy sought.

The grievance shall be presented to the
appropriate employer representative in
writing within 14 days after the occurrence of the alleged violation.

After the presentation of the grievance,
the employee and the Nurses' Association
Representative shall be offered an opportunity to meet with the appropriate
employer representative in an attempt
to settle the grievance. The decision
of the employer representative shall be
in writing and shall be transmitted to
the employee within 14 days after
receipt of the written grievance unless
extended by mutual consent.

Step 2: Arbitration
If the matter is not satisfactorily settled at Step 1 and the employee desires
to proceed with arbitration, the employee
shall serve written notice on the employer of the desire to arbitrate within
five days of receipt of the written
decision of the employer under Step 1.

If an additional step from "appropriate employer
representative" to the administrator is needed,
it should be included as Step 2 and arbitration
would become Step 3.

SUGGESTED CONTRACT LANGUAGE	BASIS FOR JUSTIFICATION	NOTATIONS

Article XIII - The Grievance Procedure (continued)

Selection of an arbitrator shall be by agreement if possible or, if the parties cannot so agree within five (5) days, from a list of five (5) arbitrators obtained by request to the Federal Mediation and Conciliation Service with the parties alternately striking names until only one name remains.

The award of the arbitrator shall be accepted as final and binding. There shall be no appeal from the arbitrator's decision by either party if such decision is within the scope of the arbitrator's authority as described below:

a. The arbitrator shall not have the power to add to, subtract from, disregard, alter or modify any of the terms of this agreement.

b. His power shall be limited to deciding whether the employer has violated any of the terms of this agreement. It is understood that any matter that is not specifically set forth in this agreement shall not be subject to arbitration.

c. In any case of discipline or discharge where the arbitrator finds that such discipline or discharge was improper the arbitrator may set aside, reduce or modify the action taken by the employer. If the penalty is set aside, reduced or otherwise changed, the arbitrator may award back pay to compensate the employee wholly or partially for any wages or other benefits lost because of the penalty.

The fees and expenses of the arbitrator, shall be shared equally by the employer and the employee.

An arbitrator can also be obtained through the American Arbitration Association, but an administrative fee is charged.

SUGGESTED CONTRACT LANGUAGE	BASIS FOR JUSTIFICATION	NOTATIONS

ARTICLE XIV
Evaluation

Written evaluations of the employee's performance will be presented at _____ intervals. A copy of the evaluation will be given to the employee and a conference will be held with the employee regarding the evaluation. If the employee does not accept the evaluation as written, the employee's exceptions to the evaluation shall be attached to and made a part of the evaluation.

ARTICLE XV
Resignation or Termination

In the event there is a need for the employee to resign, one months prior written notice will be given to the employer.

Termination or other discipline of the employee shall be only for just cause. One months prior written notice of termination will be given. Termination or other discipline of the employee is subject to the grievance procedure herein.

ARTICLE XVI
Duration

The contract shall remain in full force and effect one year from the date first written above and shall be automatically renewed on a year to year basis thereafter. Each such one year period will be a new duration period with a new effective date.

Either party may serve upon the other party a written notice of intention to amend or terminate this agreement. The notice must be served at least 60 days before the first anniversary date of the agreement or any anniversary date thereafter and must state the nature of the amend-

---

If termination is attempted by the employer without just cause, the nurse may prefer to insure several months payment of salary in lieu of use of the grievance procedure. i.e. nurse will be paid through termination date of contract.

A specific time could also be negotiated - 3 months, 6 months, or one year. SNA staff can be used for consultation.

It is not wise to negotiate for too long a period of time with the economy as unpredictable as it is. A contract for a one year period is sufficient. It is to the employee's advantage to re-negotiate each year.

SUGGESTED CONTRACT LANGUAGE

Article XVII - Duration (continued)

The parties will meet with respect to the requested amendments within 30 days of receipt of said notice.

These guidelines are a product of a joint effort by the American Nurses' Association Economic and General Welfare Department and the Council of Nurse Practitioners in the Nursing of Children.

For the employer   For the employee
By _____   By _____
   date   date

MLP:JL:jlm

Revised
5/22/74

EC-126/35¢

2,000

APPENDIX II. SAMPLE PROFESSIONAL LIABILITY POLICY

PROFESSIONAL LIABILITY POLICY
ST. PAUL FIRE AND MARINE INSURANCE COMPANY
ST. PAUL, MINNESOTA
A Capital Stock Company

SPECIMEN

DECLARATIONS

ITEM 1. Name and Address of Insured

A
G
E
N
C
Y

THE ST. PAUL
COMPANIES

Serving you around the world ... around the clock

ITEM 2. POLICY PERIOD*
FROM | TO | POLICY PREMIUM | ITEM 3. Limits of Liability
EACH CLAIM | ANNUAL AGGREGATE

*12:01 A.M. Standard time at the address of the Insured as stated herein

ITEM 4. Classification

NEW | RENEWAL

COUNTERSIGNATURE DATE | COUNTERSIGNED AT | AUTHORIZED REPRESENTATIVE

In consideration of the payment of the premium and the statements contained in the Declarations and subject to the limits of liability, exclusions, conditions and other terms of this Policy, the ST. PAUL FIRE AND MARINE INSURANCE COMPANY, herein called the Company, AGREES with the Insured named in the Declarations made a part hereof:

INSURING AGREEMENTS

A — PROFESSIONAL LIABILITY

To pay on behalf of the **Insured** all sums which the **Insured** shall become legally obligated to pay as **damages** arising out of the performance of **professional services** rendered or which should have been rendered, during the **policy period,** by the **Insured** or by any person for whose acts or omissions the **Insured** is legally responsible or any counterclaims in suit brought by the **Insured** to collect fees and the Company shall have the right and duty to defend in his name and behalf any suit against the **Insured** alleging **damages,** even if such suit is groundless, false or fraudulent; but the Company shall have the right to make such investigation and settlement of any claim or suit as may be deemed expedient by the Company.

B — SUPPLEMENTARY PAYMENTS

The Company will pay, in addition to the applicable limit of liability:
1. all expenses incurred by the Company, all costs taxed against the **Insured** in any suit defended by the Company and all interest on the entire amount of any judgment therein which accrues after entry of the judgment and before the Company has paid or tendered or deposited in court that part of the judgment which does not exceed the limit of the Company's liability thereon;

2. premiums on appeal bonds required in any such suit, premiums on bonds to release attachments in any such suit for an amount not in excess of the applicable limit of liability of this Policy, but the Company shall have no obligation to apply for or furnish any such bonds;

3. reasonable expenses incurred by the **Insured** at the Company's request, including actual loss of wages or salary (but not loss of other income not to exceed $25 per day because of his attendance at hearings or trials at such request.

C — DEFINITION OF INSURED

The word "Insured" shall mean (a) each individual and (b) the partnership corporation or professional association named in the Declarations

D — POLICY PERIOD — TERRITORY

This coverage applies to **professional services** performed during the **policy period.**

EXCLUSIONS

1. This insurance does not apply: to liability of the **Insured** as a proprietor, superintendent or executive officer of any hospital, sanitarium, clinic with bed and board facilities, laboratory or business enterprise.

CONDITIONS

A. DEFINITIONS — WHEN USED IN THIS POLICY OR ENDORSEMENTS FORMING A PART HEREOF:

"Damages" means all damages, including damages for death, which are payable because of injury to which this insurance applies.

"Professional Services" means injury, sickness, disease, death or destruction due to the rendering of or failure to render any professional service and shall be deemed to include the dispensing of drugs or medicine and the service by the **Insured** as a member of a formal accreditation or similar board or committee of a hospital or professional society;

19738 PLS Rev. 10-75 Printed in U.S.A.

B. LIMITS OF LIABILITY

The limit of liability stated in the Declarations as applicable to "each claim" is the limit of the Company's liability for loss resulting from any one claim or suit or all suits because of injury to or death of any one person. The limit of liability stated in the Declarations as "annual aggregate" is, subject to the above provision respecting "each claim", the total limit of the Company's liability during the effective policy period. Such limits of liability shall apply separately to each **Insured.**

C. INSURED'S DUTIES IN THE EVENT OF OCCURRENCE, CLAIM OR SUIT

1. Upon the **Insured** becoming aware of any alleged injury, written notice containing the fullest information obtainable with respect to the circumstances, time and place thereof, and the names and addresses of the injured and of available witnesses shall be given by or for the **Insured** to the Company or any of its authorized agents as soon as practicable.

2. If claim is made or suit is brought against the **Insured,** the **Insured** shall immediately forward to the Company every demand, notice, summons or other process received by him or his representative.

3. The **Insured** shall cooperate with the Company and, upon the Company's request, assist in making settlements, in the conduct of suits and in enforcing any right of contribution or indemnity against any person or organization who may be liable to the **Insured** because of injury, with respect to which insurance is afforded under this Policy; and the **Insured** shall attend hearings and trials and assist in securing and giving evidence and obtaining the attendance of witnesses. The **Insured** shall not, except at his own cost, voluntarily make any payment, assume any obligation or incur any expense other than for first aid to others at the time of accident.

D. ACTION AGAINST COMPANY

No action shall lie against the Company unless, as a condition precedent thereto, there shall have been full compliance with all of the terms of this Policy, nor until the amount of the **Insured's** obligation to pay shall have been finally determined either by judgment against the **Insured** after actual trial or by written agreement of the **Insured,** the claimant and the Company.

Any person or organization or the legal representative thereof who has secured such judgment or written agreement shall thereafter be entitled to recover under this Policy to the extent of the insurance afforded by this Policy. No person or organization shall have any right under this Policy to join the Company as a party to any action against the **Insured** to determine the **Insured's** liability, nor shall the Company be impleaded by the **Insured** or his legal representative. Bankruptcy or insolvency of the **Insured** or of the **Insured's** estate shall not relieve the Company of any of its obligations hereunder.

E. OTHER INSURANCE

If the **Insured** has other insurance against a loss covered by this Policy, the Company shall not be liable under this Policy for a greater proportion of such loss than the limit of liability stated in the Declarations bears to the total limit of liability of all valid and collectible insurance against such loss.

When both this insurance and other insurance apply to the loss on the same basis, whether primary, excess or contingent, the Company shall not be liable under this Policy for a greater proportion of the loss than that stated in the applicable contribution provision below:

(1) CONTRIBUTION BY EQUAL SHARES.

If all of such other valid and collectible insurance provides for contribution by equal shares, the Company shall not be liable for a greater proportion of such loss than would be payable if each insurer contributes an equal share until the share of each insurer equals the lowest applicable limit of liability under any one policy or the full amount of the loss is paid, and with respect to any amount of loss not so paid the remaining insurers then continue to contribute equal shares of the remaining amount of the loss until each such insurer has paid its limit in full or the full amount of the loss is paid.

(2) CONTRIBUTION BY LIMITS.

If any of such other insurance does not provide for contribution by equal shares, the Company shall not be liable for a greater proportion of such loss than the applicable limit of liability under this Policy for such loss bears to the total applicable limit of liability of all valid and collectible insurance against such loss.

F. SUBROGATION

In the event of any payment under this Policy the Company shall be subrogated to all the **Insured's** rights of recovery therefor against any person or organization (excluding, employees of the **Insured**) and the **Insured** shall execute and deliver instruments and papers and do whatever else is necessary to secure such rights. The **Insured** shall do nothing after loss to prejudice such rights.

G. CHANGES

Notice to any agent or knowledge possessed by any agent or by any other person shall not affect a waiver or a change in any part of this Policy or estop the Company from asserting any right under the terms of this Policy; nor shall the terms of this Policy be waived or changed, except by endorsement issued to form a part of this Policy.

H. ASSIGNMENT

Assignment of interest under this Policy shall not bind the Company until its consent is endorsed hereon; if, however, the Named **Insured** shall die, such insurance as is afforded by this Policy shall apply (1) to the Named **Insured's** legal representative, as the Named **Insured,** but only while acting within the scope of his duties as such, and (2) with respect to the property of the Named **Insured,** to the person having proper temporary custody thereof, as Insured, but only until the appointment and qualification of the legal representative.

I. CANCELLATION

This Policy may be cancelled by the Named **Insured** by surrender thereof to the Company or any of its authorized agents or by mailing to the Company written notice stating when thereafter the cancellation shall be effective. This Policy may be cancelled by the Company by mailing to the Named **Insured** at the address shown in this Policy, written notice stating when not less than ten days thereafter such cancellation shall be effective. The mailing of notice as aforesaid shall be sufficient proof of notice. The time of surrender or the effective date and hour of cancellation stated in the notice shall become the end of the policy period. Delivery of such written notice either by the Named **Insured** or by the Company shall be equivalent to mailing.

If the Named **Insured** cancels, earned premium shall be computed in accordance with the customary short rate table and procedure. If the Company cancels, earned premium shall be computed pro rata. Premium adjustment may be made either at the time cancellation is effected or as soon as practicable after cancellation becomes effective, but payment or tender of unearned premium is not a condition of cancellation.

J. DECLARATIONS

By acceptance of this Policy, the Named **Insured** agrees that the statements in the Declarations are his agreements and representations, that this Policy is issued in reliance upon the truth of such representations and that this Policy embodies all agreements existing between himself and the Company or any of its agents relating to this insurance.

K. SPECIAL STATUTES

Any and all provisions of this Policy which are in conflict with the statutes of the State wherein this Policy is issued are understood, declared and acknowledged by this Company to be amended to conform to such statutes.

PROVISIONS REQUIRED BY LAW TO BE STATED IN THIS POLICY: — "This Policy is issued under and in pursuance of the laws of the State of Minnesota, relating to Guaranty Surplus and Special Reserve Funds." Chapter 437, General Laws of 1909.

IN WITNESS WHEREOF, the ST. PAUL FIRE AND MARINE INSURANCE COMPANY has caused this Policy to be signed by its President and a Secretary and countersigned on the Declarations page by a duly authorized representative of the Company.

Secretary.   *President.*

SPECIAL EXCEPTIONS

Wisconsin exceptions:

1. Paragraph 1 of Condition C — entitled "Insured's Duties in the Event of Occurrence, Claim or Suit" is amended to read:

Insured's Duties in the Event of Occurrence, Claim or Suit

(1) In the event of an **occurrence**, written notice containing particulars sufficient to identify the **Insured** and also reasonably obtainable information with respect to the time, place and circumstances thereof, and the names and addresses of the injured and of available witnesses, shall be given by or for the **Insured** to the Company or any of its authorized agents within 20 days following the date of the occurrence; provided, that failure to give such notice within the time specified shall not invalidate any claim made by the **Insured** if it shall be shown not to have been reasonably possible to give such notice within the prescribed time and that such notice was given as soon as reasonably possible. The Named **Insured** shall promptly take at his expense all reasonable steps to prevent other bodily injury or property damage from arising out of the same or similar conditions, but such expense shall not be recoverable under this Policy.

2. Condition G entitled "Changes" is amended to read:

Changes

The terms of this Policy shall not be changed, except by endorsement issued to form a part of this Policy. Knowledge of an agent of the Company at the time this Policy is issued or an application made shall be knowledge of the Company, and any fact which breaches a condition of the Policy and is known to the agent when the Policy is issued or the application made shall not void the Policy or defeat a recovery thereon in the event of loss.

3. The following change is hereby made to Condition I, Cancellation:

Cancellation

This Policy may be cancelled by the Named **Insured** by surrender thereof to the Company or any of its Authorized Agents or by mailing to the Company written notice stating when thereafter the cancellation shall be effective. This Policy may be cancelled by the Company by mailing to the Named **Insured** at the address shown in this Policy, written notice stating when not less than 30 days thereafter such cancellation shall be effective. The mailing of notice as aforesaid shall be sufficient proof of notice. The time of surrender, or the effective date and hour of cancellation stated in the notice shall become the end of the policy period. If the Company elects not to renew this Policy, it shall mail to the Named **Insured**, at the address shown in the Policy, written notice of such nonrenewal not less than thirty days prior to the termination or expiration of this Policy. The mailing of notice as aforesaid shall be sufficient proof of notice.

If the Named **Insured** cancels, earned premium shall be computed in accordance with the customary short rate table and procedure. If the Company cancels, earned premium shall be computed pro rata. Premium adjustment may be made either at the time cancellation is effected or as soon as practicable after cancellation becomes effective, but payment or tender of unearned premium is not a condition of cancellation.

4. The following paragraph is added to Condition J entitled "Declarations":

No oral or written statement, representation or warranty made by the **Insured** or in his behalf in the negotiation of this Policy shall be deemed material or defeat or avoid the Policy, unless such statement, representation or warranty was false and made with intent to deceive, or unless the matter misrepresented or made a warranty increased the risk or contributed to the loss. No breach of a warranty in this Policy shall defeat or avoid this Policy unless the breach of such warranty increased the risk at the time of the loss, or contributed to the loss, or existed at the time of the loss.

Carefully note Condition requiring Immediate Notice of Every Occurrence, Claim and Suit.

INDEX